AVISSON YOUNG ADULT SERIES

Go, Girl!
Young Women Superstars of Pop Music

Jacqueline Robb

Avisson Press, Inc.
Greensboro

First edition
Printed in the United States of America

Library of Congress Cataloging-in-Publication Data
Robb, Jacqueline, 1964-
    Go, Girl!: young women superstars of pop music / Jacqueline Robb.-- 1st ed.
       p. cm. -- (Avisson young adult series)
    Includes index.
    ISBN 1-888105-44-5 (lib. bdg.)
    1. Singers--Biography--Juvenile literature. 2. Women Singers--Biography--Juvenile literature. [1. Singers. 2. Women--Biography.] I. Title. II. Series.

ML400 .R73 2000
782.42164'092'2--dc21
[B]

                      00-033200

Photo credits: All photos are from AP/Wide World Photos.

Contents

Britney rehearsing for the MTV Video Music Awards at New
York's Lincoln Center in September, 1999.

Britney Spears

BRITNEY SPEARS IS pop music's Cinderella, a small town girl who has hit the big time in a big way. A down-home country girl bursting with confidence, energy and strong values, Britney hit the pop music scene with her debut album, *Baby One More Time*, which included the monster hit singles "Baby One More Time," "Sometimes" and "Drive Me Crazy."

But Britney is no flash-in-the-pan, no overnight sensation. She has actually been working in show business since she was a small child. She has definitely paid her dues and then some.

Britney Jean Spears was born on December 2, 1981, in Kentwood, Louisiana. Although her parents, Lynne, a teacher and Jamie, a foreman at a construction company, already had their hands full with their five-year-old son, they were delighted to welcome their dark-blond, brown-eyed daughter. They spelled her first name B-r-i-t-n-e-y because, as Britney tells it, "My mom spelled it the way it sounded."

· With a population of 2,500, Kentwood is a place where the birth of a new baby is cause for a total town celebration. Britney remembers her hometown as a place of simple beauty and old-fashioned goodness, a quiet, slow-moving town filled with a sense of timelessness. "It looks like something out a movie," she told *Tiger Beat* magazine. "Everybody knows everybody. For some reason, all my mom's friends had kids at the same time, so it was like I had all these sisters."

But even at a young age, Britney sought out the spotlight. From the time she was able to talk, she was singing, and from the moment she could walk, she was dancing and doing flips.

Britney's parents were amazed at their daughter's strong, clear voice, and they encouraged her constantly. Her first public performance took place at the local Baptist Church, which her family attended each week—she sang "What Child Is This?" at a Christmas service, and her audience was totally awed by her abilities. Although she was a mere four years old, she was able to recognize that her singing brought people pleasure—everyone always smiled their approval at her.

It was clear to everyone that Britney loved attention, and clamored for the spotlight; but also that she had a talent that made people want to watch and listen to her. As Britney grew, her love of music and performing grew as well. Although she experienced a few bouts of shyness and nerves, they quickly disappeared when she stepped in front of an audience. "My mom would have company, and I would be dancing and doing flips," she told *16* magazine. "As long as there was someone watching, I felt like I could do anything."

To make the most of Brit's natural gifts, her mom did what millions of parents across the country do for their daughters—she enrolled Britney in dance class. For two years, little Britney devoted herself to her jazz, ballet and tap classes. Her mom Lynne drove her back and forth to class in New Orleans. Britney was dedicated to dancing, always pushing herself to learn new steps and show them off once she had perfected them.

Britney's teachers noticed she was strong and extremely flexible, and they suggested to Lynne that Britney might want to pursue gymnastics. Britney "jumped" at the chance. "Doing gymnastics was so much fun," Britney told *Teen Beat*. "I had the best time doing those flips. My mom would drive me for an hour, one way, to get to gymnastics because she knew how much I loved it."

But while Britney flourished in performance gymnastics, she discovered early on that she didn't like the tough harsh world of competitive gymnastics. Early exposure to world-famous coach Bela Karolyi—the man who trained Olympic gymnast Keri Strug—convinced her that while she might love gymnastics, it wouldn't be a career for her. "I went to Bela's camp in Houston, Texas," she told *16* magazine. "I started working so hard—but I also started to cry when I had to go to class there. Everyone there was so over the top. I missed the fun of it—I was good at gymnastics because it had been fun, but it got to the point where I didn't want to do it anymore."

Britney returned to the things she loved most—and the things that came naturally to her: singing and dancing. At home, she spent lots of time gazing out of her bedroom window, dreaming about her future goals—Brit wanted to sing for millions of people and to make the whole world smile.

By the time Britney was eight, she knew exactly what she wanted in life—but getting it was another story. The answer came from another "Brit"—one of Britney's closest friends from gymnastics. "Brittany's mom had heard about an open call audition for something called the Mickey Mouse Club," Britney told *Teen Machine*. The two Brits begged their moms to drive them to Atlanta, where the audition was being held.

When the girls reached Atlanta, they faced total pandemonium—hundreds of girls and boys, between the ages of 10 and 17 had turned up; many had driven thousands of miles from all over the South. The Mickey

Mouse Club was a very popular show on The Disney Channel, a comedy-variety show that gave its young stars the chance to show off their singing, acting and dancing skills.

Britney did very well at her first audition—well enough to make it down to the wire as one of that day's finalists. At the end of the day, Britney was poised to take a spot on The Mickey Mouse Club, but it was not to be. "The producers thought I was too young," Britney told *SuperStars*. "I was so disappointed I couldn't believe it."

The producers and writers of the Mickey Mouse Club all loved Brit, and were wowed by her talent, but they agreed the perky eight-year-old was too young to handle the pressure of the grueling performance and rehearsal schedules; normally, the youngest cast members were ten and eleven. They sat down with Britney and her mom and explained their feelings, and stressed their confidence in Britney's abilities. They urged Lynne to take Britney to New York City, where they knew of an agent and an entertainment lawyer who could manage Britney's future. Britney and her family were floored by the prospect. "Where I'm from, you don't say, 'I'm going to New York,'" Britney told *SuperTeen*. "People were like, 'What are you doing?' It was totally unheard of." At first, Lynne and Jamie decided against the trip, but Britney was determined, and already delighted at the prospect of heading north. "I was like, 'Please, mom, take me!'" she told *Tiger Beat*. "I wanted to go to New York so bad. So I just kept asking my mom and dad, and they believed in me enough to do it."

That summer, Lynne and Britney packed their bags and flew off to the Big Apple. She immediately jumped in to her career—she studied at the Professional Performing Arts School and at The Dance Center, a well-known Off-Broadway organization devoted to dance instruction and the arts. Soon she made her mark with a role in the 1991 Off-Broadway comedy *Ruthless*, based on the 1956 horror film *The Bad Seed*. "I was playing the lead every single night," she told *16* Magazine. "Plus I was keeping up with my studies—I was working really hard." In addition to the play, she was also appearing in TV ads for Mitsubishi cars and Mall BBQ Sauce. She spent two years in New York City before returning home.

It was around this same time that Britney made her first foray into the national arena—via the hit TV talent show *Star Search*. Brit auditioned for the show in Baton Rouge, Louisiana and nabbed a spot in the spotlight. She traveled to Los Angeles where the show was filmed, and performed her song, dressed in a black velvet dress with a huge white ribbon in her hair. "I couldn't believe my mama dressed me in that outfit!" Brit exclaimed to *All-Stars* magazine. Obviously the judges didn't mind it, because she won her first competition—unfortunately, she lost the following week. But being part of Star Search reminded Britney of how much being in the music business meant to her.

A few weeks before her 11th birthday, Britney urged her mom to take her on a trip to Orlando, Florida, where the Mickey Mouse Club was filmed—she was determined to grab a spot on the show. This time, the producers couldn't say no; she was definitely ready to wear the mouse ears.

Britney made her MMC debut in 1992, along with several other talented stars of the future, like Christina Aguilera, Nikki DeLoach (of Innosense) and Justin Timberlake. Other MMC alumni, like JC Chasez and Keri Russell, would also hit it huge after first achieving fame on the Club. Britney enjoyed her experience at the Mickey Mouse Club—she was a cast member for two years before the show was finally cancelled. "I was eleven, and I was the baby on the show, so people catered to me," she recalled to America Online. "And goodness, being in Disney World alone was so much fun for me. But I was also learning a lot—I learned exactly how much I love to sing."

Britney was 13 when the Mickey Mouse Club was cancelled. She had been performing in one way or another for most of her young life. So she took a break from the spotlight—she returned home to Kentwood, went back to school and rebuilt her relationships with friends. But she was dissatisfied. "I wasn't happy hanging around at home," she told *Tiger Beat* magazine. "I wanted to see the world, and make music and do all these wonderful things."

Around that same time, Britney got word that a girl group was forming down in Orlando, Florida—her friend from MMC, Nikki DeLoach, had already signed on. The group would be called Innosense, and Brit thought it might be fun to be a part of a group. But she soon realized that she really wanted to pursue a solo career. "I realized that was what I wanted," she told *SuperStars* magazine. "And from then on, everything became really clear."

With the re-emergence of pop music, many people in the music industry were creating and promoting young, energetic performers—and Brit's entertainment lawyer, Larry Rudolph, urged her to make a demo tape and send it to him. She did as he suggested, and her took the demo to Jive Records. The rest, as they say, is history.

But the tape was only an introduction—the executives at Jive had to meet Britney to make sure she could really sing, that the tape hadn't been doctored to create the soulful, powerful sound they'd heard. Soon Britney was back in New York, auditioning for the creative staff at Jive. "I felt so weird, standing there in the conference room, basically singing for my life," she told *Billboard* magazine. "But you have to take your opportunities wherever you can, and make the most of them."

Britney did just that, and her audience couldn't believe what they heard. They signed Britney immediately. "I thought, this was too good to be true!" she told *Entertainment Weekly*.

Teaming up with Jive records was the smartest thing Britney could have done—the company had built a strong reputation guiding The Backstreet Boys' career, and they were certainly in a position to help Britney achieve the same success.

Britney was flown to Sweden, where she met with the legendary producer and song writer Eric Foster White, who'd created musical magic for artists like Boyzone and Whitney Houston. Together with Sweden's Cheiron Production team, producer Max Martin and Per Magnusson, the majority of the recording took place in an astounding 10 days. "It was hard work," Britney told *16* magazine. "But we always took time off to goof around and act stupid."

The star-to-be was caught in a total whirlwind of work—every day she went into the studio, and gave her music everything she had. After putting down her vocal tracks, Britney returned to New York City, where the final recording sessions took place. She was thrilled to be back, happy to be in the city she considered her "adopted home."

By mid-1998, everyone involved in Brit's debut album gave it a listen and realized they had a serious hit on their hands. To build momentum around the album, Jive created an ingenious marketing plan, setting up a toll-free number so that fans could call in and listen to snippets of music, and well as to interviews with Britney herself. Jive Records also jumped into cyberland, setting up a Web page that featured interviews, pictures and even more music snippets.

Britney also began working hard to promote the album. She flew to Singapore for a promotional concert, and came away invigorated. The audience loved Britney and she returned the sentiment. "I was so nervous because it was my first performance," she told *Teen Machine* magazine. "But it was just perfect. The people and the country were beautiful."

After returning home from Singapore, Britney immediately began another road trip—the home grown kind. Three months before the release of the single "Baby One More Time," Britney began an intense mall tour of middle America. With two dancers to back her up (and to pass out free cassette samplers to all in attendance), Britney set off on a 28-day jaunt sponsored by magazines like *YM* and *Teen*.

Britney was totally excited by the mall tour, and she used the opportunity to perfect her stage show, integrating precise, eye-catching choreography with her pumped up sound. She also learned about the downside of the music biz—long weeks away from friends and family, traveling on a tour, lack of sleep, endless movies on the VCR and long, long hours. "The only downside to this is being away from your family," she told *Teen Beat* magazine. To stay bonded with her family, Britney spent hours on her cell phone, directly connected to Kentwood. "I don't know how much money I spend on phone bills," she told *SuperTeen* magazine. "I just call up my mom and say, 'Mama, what are you doin'? I don't care what time of day it is, I just was to hear your voice!'"

Britney also began to visit radio stations across the country. She wowed radio bigwigs with her sweet and sincerely go-get-'em personality. With pop radio firmly in her corner, Britney was positioned for success. Now all the radio world needed was a hit single—and one was definitely on its way. "Baby One More Time" was released to radio stations on November 3, 1998, and immediately scored on the Billboard charts—its hypnotic beat and catchy lyrics combined to create an instant hit. On December 28, the single went gold. Britney still remembers the first time she heard her song on the radio: "I was home—I'd just gotten off an airplane," she told

Bop magazine. "I was in the car heading home, when—oh my goodness—it came on. It was so weird. I started screaming like a big goob."

Of course, the video for "Baby One More Time" was also a smash—but it also brought Brit her first taste of controversy. Set in a high school (it was shot at Venice High School in California), featuring Britney and her dancers dressed in provocative schoolgirl uniforms, the video attracted tons of attention—some of it less than positive.

But most of Britney's fans, both adults and kids, responded well to the video, and soon, a legion of young female fans began showing up at Britney's shows, dressed in plaid skirts, pigtails, and pom-poms.

That winter, Britney took to the road again, this time as the opening act for the boy group 'N Sync. The group was hugely popular in the US, which made it a smart move from a business standpoint, but more importantly to Britney, two of the 'N Sync-ers were old friends, Justin Timberlake and JC Chasez from the Mickey Mouse Club. That helped get Britney through the back-breaking tour schedule—and some of the other, more unpleasant things she faced on the road. "It's not easy being an opening act for these guys," she told *Billboard* magazine. "There are all these girls in the audience, and they're there to see 'N Sync. But ultimately, I'm able to win them over. I have guy dancers, and believe me, that helps!"

If the release of the single created a fanfare, then the release of the album created pure Brit-mania. The debut album, *Baby One More Time*, was released on January 13, 1999, and fueled by the high energy and enthusiasm of the first single, the album soared to number one on the charts. It remained there for a week, then dropped—but within four weeks it was back on top, smashing the nearest competitor, *The Miseducation Of Lauryn Hill*, by a whopping 70,000 CDs.

Britney's fans were delighted with the album; it was fun, fresh and full of energy. "A lot of the songs deal with love and relationships," Britney told *SuperTeen* magazine. "And a lot of them are just so much fun."

The next single, "Sometimes," also climbed the charts, and made the summer of '99 a pure Britney summer. And her third, "Drive Me Crazy" was a total smash—it graced the soundtrack of the movie *Drive Me Crazy*, which starred Melissa Joan Hart of *Sabrina the Teenage Witch* fame.

Of course, Britney was proud of her album, it represented years of hard work and determination. But Brit also looked forward to the day when she could do her own song-writing. Because she's a young artist, Britney didn't get a chance to write any of the songs on *Baby One More Time*, but she's already working on tunes for the next album, and her first single, "I'm So Curious," appeared on the B-side of "Sometimes." "When I was first signed to the record label, there were producers left and right, bringing me songs to sing," she told *16* magazine. "But all along, I was writing on my own. 'I'm So Curious' is all about a girl and a guy, and he likes her, and she likes him, but she doesn't know if she should go for it and ask him out. So she says, 'I'm so curious' like about how it's all going to turn out."

With her talent, determination and will to succeed, Britney Spear's star is destined to shine brightly for years to come. The only question is, will it be shining in the music world or the TV and movie world?

Although she's reached an enormous audience with her music, she's also been involved in acting since she was a child—and if you've ever caught any of the Mickey Mouse Club re-runs, you know she's got tremendous abilities in that realm too.

Britney's also working with several production companies to create a series of her own. And of course, she has her eyes on the movies. "I would definitely love to get into films," she told America Online. "That would be fun! I've already done regional commercials and theater, so I have some experience. It would be an exciting thing to do."

It's no surprise that Britney might want to expand her career horizons. After all, she's been quoted as admiring Madonna, who's known for her chameleon qualities, reinventing herself from pop icon to movie star and back again. And Britney's voice has already been compared to Madonna's—a true compliment for her. "I totally respect and admire Madonna," she told *USA Today*. "She's grown so much as an artist, and she's always changing. I'd love to do a duet with her one day—I think that would be a real shocker to everyone."

Although her career and her future obviously mean the world to Britney, at heart she's just a normal teenage girl, who still enjoys doing the types of things most teenagers do. She's a shop-a-holic ("I'm crazy when it comes to shopping," she told *16* magazine. "Just let me loose in a store and I'll go wild.") and she loves gossiping with her friends, hanging out at home with her family and meeting famous celebrities, like her crush object, Ben Affleck. "He's soooo cute!" she told *SuperTeen* magazine, sounding like any normal teen girl.

Though success may have its ups and downs, Britney Spears is definitely having the time of her life. "No one can ever take this time away from me," she told *Tiger Beat* magazine. "I'll always have this to remember, no matter what happens." But there's no doubt, no matter what happens, Britney will always see her name in lights. A Cinderella superstar would have it no other way.

Shania performs at the Country Music Association Awards show in Nashville, Tennesse in September of 1999.

Shania Twain

SHANIA TWAIN IS no ordinary country singer. Although her glorious voice can growl and belt out a sad country tune, Shania long ago set her sights on changing the face of country, bringing it into the '90s with style and serious flare. By doing so, she turned herself into that rarity—the country singer with pop music appeal, a superstar who can cross all musical styles and genres.

But don't let the glamour and glitter of fame fool you; Ms. Twain is a true blue country girl down to the bottom of her heart; a child of the land who faced bitter hardships as she grew up in her native Timmins, Ontario, Canada. She's a strong-willed woman who has triumphed to become one of the most famous singers in the world today.

Shania, born Eileen Twain, made her first entrance into the world in Windsor, a suburban city in southern Ontario. When she was two, her mother, Sharon, moved Eileen and her older sister to Timmins, a gold-mining outpost that was home to those who loved the outdoor life. Her step-father, Jerry, who'd married Sharon when Eileen was still a child, found it difficult to make ends meet—he logged timber occasionally, but spent most of his time prospecting for gold, trying to strike it rich. (Shania's biological father, Clarence Edwards, left the family when she was a baby—she's had no contact with him throughout her life). Shania remembers the poverty of her early years very well. "Sometimes, we'd each get a potato apiece for the day," she told *Country America* Magazine. "To help feed the family, my father taught us to kill our own food. My job was to set the rabbit snares."

She was always hungry. Shania remembers bringing two slices of bread, coated with mayonnaise or mustard, as a sandwich for lunch at school. She became obsessed with her family's poverty, convinced that if anyone knew, they'd come and take her away from her parents. "I was the kid who went to school without a lunch," Shania told *Country America.* "It was hard. I'd judge other kids by their lunches. If they had cake, I thought they must be rich."

Despite her hardships, little Eileen found things to sing about—and sing she did. From the age of three, Eileen constantly surprised her family by showing off her amazing voice. By the age of eight, she was singing and playing the guitar, and by ten, she was writing her own songs. "I liked to escape my personal life through my music," she told *Rolling Stone*. "Music was all I ever did. I would spend hours with my guitar, writing songs and singing away for hours. I would play till my fingers bruised."

By now, the Twain family had grown, with four kids to feed and clothe, and Eileen's parents, especially her mother, were convinced that her singing might be a way to bring in money for the family. "She knew I was talented, and she lived with the hope that my abilities were my chance to do something special," she told *Country America*.

Back then, young Eileen had absolutely no intention of becoming a major singing star. Although she loved to sing, she was too shy to ever imagine facing an audience by herself. She dreamed of being a back-up singer to some famous performer, or of writing songs for others to sing—she couldn't imagine calling attention to herself, since she'd spent so many years learning how to hide in the background to avoid detection. But her mom had other ideas.

Before long, Sharon Twain was dragging Eileen to community centers, nursing homes, hospitals and other organizations that would give her daughter a chance to perform. Soon, Sharon discovered the Canadian nightclub scene—after 1:00 AM, when alcohol was no longer sold, young people could enter the clubs, and Sharon and Jerry would ask the club owners to let their daughter sing. "I hated that," she told *The Chicago Sun-Times*. "I didn't feel like singing at that time of night at all." But Eileen did well. Dressed in fringe vests and denim skirts, she wowed the tough crowds, although she was still really a little girl.

Soon, Eileen Twain was a famous name in the small towns surrounding Toronto, Canada. Her mother encouraged her to take voice lessons, and by the time she was 16, Eileen was a full-fledged member of a rock band called Longshot. Looking back, of course, Longshot was really just a group that played for high school parties, and it earned little money, so Eileen supplemented her income with part time jobs. "I worked hard," she recalled to *Rolling Stone*. "But I didn't mind it. I just knew I had to help out the family."

Despite her long working hours, Eileen continued to make music. She was learning to be more comfortable and natural on stage. Even though she still thought of herself as a tomboy, the truth was she was turning into a beautiful young woman who could command a stage.

After graduating from high school, Eileen's mom Sharon set out to find a manager for her talented daughter. Mary Bailey was her choice, and although she was inexperienced, she knew that Eileen belonged in

Nashville, Tennessee. Eileen disagreed—she considered herself a rock singer. She and Mary parted ways, and Eileen continued singing in local clubs.

In 1987, Sharon, Jerry and their youngest child Darryl were in a serious car accident. Sharon and Jerry were killed instantly, and Darryl survived with minor injuries. Eileen was 21 years old, and her entire world was turned upside down.

Before she had time to grieve about the loss of her parents, Eileen had to get to work taking care of her three siblings—Carrie, who was 18, Mark who was 14, and 13-year-old Darryl. With her parents gone, the financial situation was more dire than ever before. "I didn't have time to grieve for myself," she told *USA Weekend*. "Taking care of my siblings was a blessing in disguise, because it was a total distraction from grief. Boy oh boy, did I ever get strong."

Eileen's former almost-manager, Mary, helped the young woman find work singing at the Deerhurst Resort, about 150 miles north of Toronto. The job paid very well, and Eileen was able to buy a house for herself and her younger brothers. Just as importantly to her, Eileen was again learning how to be a professional singer. "I got to learn about staging, choreography and production," Eileen told *Rolling Stone*. "My biggest development as a performer came from Deerhurst."

When her younger brothers graduated from high
school, Eileen was free of family responsibilities, and she
didn't quite know what to do next. All she knew was she
still had the dreams, the determination and the drive to
make it in the music business. Once again, she turned to
Mary Bailey, and Mary didn't disappoint. Once again, she
sent tapes of Eileen to Nashville. This time, Nashville
responded, and soon Eileen, now 26 years old, flew down
to meet with several record producers. She recorded
several demos, and it wasn't long before Mercury
Records signed the Canadian singer with the beautiful,
strong voice.

It was at Mercury Records that Eileen Twain
reinvented herself fully. When producers suggested she
should adopt a stage name, she remembered a woman
from Deerhurst Resort who went by the name of
Shania—an Ojibwa Indian name which translated to "I'm
On My Way!" "That's how I felt then," she told *Country
America.* "It seemed very right, I thought, to celebrate
with that name." Almost as important to her was the fact
that her step-father Jerry was part Ojibwa Indian, and
Eileen thought it was fitting to pay tribute to him that
way.

The newly-named Shania was thrilled to be working
on her first album, but her excitement disappeared when
she realized she would have very little say in the songs

that would appear on it, and she became despondent when she learned that the record company had no interest at all in the song she herself had written. "I wasn't happy," she told *Rolling Stone*. "But I didn't protest. I wanted to be successful, and I thought this was the way."

Another thing Shania did to "be successful" was to create a totally phony identity on her first bio, which is an introduction to the press sent out by record companies. In it, Shania invented stories about her childhood, suggesting that she was "foreman" of a crew that planted trees. She also lied when she said that no one she knew growing up knew about her dreams of becoming a singer. For whatever reason, at this point and time, Shania had decided to become someone else entirely.

The first single from Shania's first album was called "What Made You Say That?" and it totally bombed—it stalled at number fifty-five on the country singles chart and never received any radio play. In fact, the only one who seemed to like Shania's music was noted actor Sean Penn, who directed the video for her second single, "Dance With The One That Brought You."

But there was one other person who thought Shania was something special—someone who watched her "What Made You Say That?" video and thought he'd found the superstar he'd been looking for. His name was Mutt Lange, and he was, at the time, one of the most successful rock 'n roll producers in the world, having created music for everyone from Def Leppard to AC/DC to Bryan Adams. "I loved everything he ever did," Shania told *Rolling Stone.* "I thought he was the most amazing, creative guy. Once we got to know each other, and started talking to each other, our conversations would last for three hours."

Slowly, as Shania grew to trust Mutt more and more, she started playing him to songs she'd written herself, an upbeat tune called "Any Man Of Mine," and a gentle ballad called "Home Ain't Where The Heart Is (Anymore)". He loved them, and was shocked when she told him her record company had discouraged her from recording them.

In June of 1993, Shania made her first appearance at Fan Fair in Nashville, but more importantly for her, Mutt Lange came to town to discuss Shania's career with Mercury Records. Till then, she wasn't even sure if a second album would be released; now, it looked like that was a done deal. And as the two got to know each other even more, it was obvious that there were romantic sparks flying between them. "I was definitely attracted to him immediately," she told *Rolling Stone* Magazine. "And I felt safe with him too. I trusted him totally."

Mutt was brought in to Mercury Nashville to produce Shania's second album—this time there would be no mistakes. Shania would be given free rein to record the song she had written on her own and with him. To make the record company even happier, he agreed to take on the costs of making the album, as long as Mercury paid him a larger cut of the profits (if there were any, of course).

Shania was thrilled to get another chance at hitting the big time, and she began to work on the second album with total abandon. All around her, country music was becoming a stronger presence in the entertainment world, and there were plenty of new and exciting artists on the scene, but Shania concentrated on her own work. "I didn't want to just do what other people were doing," she told *Country America*. "I wanted to make an album of my own, with my own music."

Shania and Mutt flew to London, England, where they could write and work together without distractions. "We ended up writing half the album before we became romantically involved," she told *Rolling Stone* magazine. But it was inevitable they would fall in love—Shania thrived under the older man's constant attention and praise, and the work they did together was amazing. "It was a force that brought us together," she said.

Six months after the pair met at Fan Fair, on December 28, 1993, Mutt and Shania sneaked away and got married. "He really is Mr. Wonderful," she told *Country America*. The marriage brought Shania total happiness, but it was the song writing the pair did together that really energized her. "Writing is like coloring," she told *Rolling Stone*. "Kids like to color. They don't need a reason to color, they just like it. They're totally open to being creative. That's how I think about songwriting. It's a chance to create."

Mercury Records released Shania's second album, *The Woman In Me,* but they had no idea what a hit they had on their hands. Although it received mixed reviews from the music critics, the fans went crazy over it. This album was pure Shania from start to finish—her style, her attitude and her words. With Mutt's help, she created something very special, and she never forgot to remind people how much she owed to his producing genius. "He's the producer of my dreams and the love of my life," she told *Country America*. "What more could any girl ask for?"

As the album, powered by the singles "Who's Bed Have Your Boots Been Under?" and "Any Man Of Mine," slowly climbed the charts, Shania received the first round of serious criticism, suggesting that Mutt was more responsible for the album's success then anyone was letting on. Critics compared her first album with *The Woman In Me*, and found too many differences to ignore. Many naysayers began to report that Mutt's producing genius had actually "created" this new voice, suggesting that Shania was only a puppet, mouthing his sound. Shania was furious at the very suggestion. "It's all me," she told *Rolling Stone* magazine. "These songs are as country, or as rock, or as pop as they are because that's what I am. I pick everything I wear, everything I do, and I'm directing myself artistically."

Shania was also soundly criticized for baring her trim stomach and showing off her midriff—something that country singers simply did not do. In fact, Country Music Television barely played her "Who's Bed Have Your Boots Been Under?" video due to what was called Shania's "gyrating." "Big deal! So I bare my midriff!" Shania said to *Rolling Stone*. "What's everyone so upset about? It's my stomach!"

The truth was, Shania's tummy-baring style was all image—in reality, she was still the shy tomboy she'd always been. "In public, I only wear a bathing suit with a wrap around it," she told *Country America*. "I'm not one for showing off anything."

By 1995, Shania was so hot it was downright scary. "My head is spinning!" she told *USA Weekend*. And as well it should—Shania had beat out Garth Brooks as country's biggest selling artist. That year, her appearance at Fan Fair drove her audience into a frenzy. Fans were totally crazy for Shania, her tough-girl attitude and her pop-star glamour. "It's about personality," she told *USA*

Weekend. "You have to be different, which is kinda what I did."

One way in which Shania was totally different was in her refusal to tour—something that totally shocked country fans, who are used to huge concert tours from their favorite performers. Once again, critics suggested that reason she wouldn't tour was because she couldn't tour, that her voice had really been fabricated in the studio. Shania had a deeper reason for avoiding the road; she wanted her show to be the biggest and the best, and since she was still considered a newcomer, she didn't think she would make that big of an impression with her live shows. She wanted to wait until she could really blow her audience away.

But not touring didn't mean not traveling. Shania traveled all over the US, meeting fans, signing autographs and posing for pictures. She was impressed by all of her fans, but especially the young women. "I always tell my fans that's it's important to just be yourself, to be who you really are," she told *Country America.* "That's the message in my music too, and I think they really respond to that."

Shania's homeland Canada was also impressed with their native daughter, and in the fall of 1995, Shania picked up a slew of Canadian Country Music Awards. Later that year, she won a Grammy for Best Country

Album, and in April of 1996, she won Academy Of Country Music Awards for Best New Female Vocalist and Album Of The Year. Shania took them all home, but she took success in stride. "I don't make a living winning these things," she told the audience at the Canadian Country Music Awards. "I make my living singing."

And make a living she did—Shania had sold over ten million copies of *The Woman In Me*. It would be hard to match that success, but Shania was ready to get back to work on her third album. "I can't say I'm feeling pressure," she told *Country Song Round-Up* magazine. "I'm just keeping my fingers crossed." The first single from the new CD was "Love Gets Me Every Time." Like the singles that came before it, it soared to the top of the country charts.

But with her new album, *Come On Over,* Shania was determined to do something few country artists had successfully done—to bridge the gap between pop music and country music, and to become a true crossover sensation. She accomplished that feat with "You're Still The One," a ballad that had the power to blow around the boundaries between the music genres. "I love all kinds of music," Shania told *Rolling Stone.* "I get a real thrill thinking I'm reaching fans who listen to all kinds of music."

Unfortunately, as Shania crossed-over, many of her

country fans began to turn away from her. Once again, she received criticism from some of the more conservative people in the music industry. Shania couldn't have cared less about the criticism, but she assured country fans in *Country Weekly* magazine, "I'm not leaving country music. I'll always be country, and I'll always think of myself as a country singer."

Shania was determined to not pay attention to the critics, and to put all her energy into her concert tour. This time, she had the clout, the money and the star power to do it right! "I'm concentrating on planning my show, and believe me, it's physically demanding," she told *Rolling Stone.*

And demanding it was—and utterly fabulous in every way. Shania's 1998 concert tour proved her critics wrong. She wowed the crowd, putting on one of the most powerful, energetic and exciting shows of the year. Suddenly, Shania's critics were nowhere to be found—newspapers were calling her "a rebel," a performer with "presence, charm and great songs to back her up," a woman with "no nonsense determination and boundless energy." She had won them all over.

Even when she was on the road, she stayed connected to her charity work with Second Harvest Food Bank and it's Kids Café Program, designed to feed poverty-stricken young people. Shania well remembered the days when she was not a powerful superstar, when she was eating those mustard sandwiches. "I know what it's like to grow up without breakfast, lunch or dinner," she told *USA Weekend*. "People have pride, and they hide it, but it goes on everyday. I hope programs like this can help make sure no other kid goes hungry again."

That year, Shania was invited to join Mariah Carey, Celine Dion, Gloria Estefan and Aretha Franklin for a special TV show, *VH1's Divas Live*. There was no doubt, to Shania, nor to anyone else, that she was one of the biggest musical stars in the galaxy. "What amazing women," Shania said to *USA Today*. "I'm honored to be in the same room with them."

Despite her awesome success and amazing popularity, Shania remains a truly genuine, good-hearted and spiritually-centered woman. She credits her marriage for giving her a firm foundation, and she deeply loves the man who helped her achieve her fame (while he himself remains firmly behind the scenes). Shania also loves spending time at home, with her dogs and her horses, where she is comfortable. "I'm not really experiencing fame," she told *USA Weekend*. "I did think it would be more glamorous—having your hair down, your make-up done, having someone shopping for your clothes. But when you get down to it, I think I'm happier just being by myself at home, taking a nice long bath, or being with my husband cooking some dinner for us. That might not be glamorous, but it's a happy life."

Brandy performs during the 26th Annual American Music Awards in Los Angeles in January of 1999.

Brandy

A SOULFUL R&B songstress; a successful TV star; a major movie maven in the making; a role model; a diva; a grounded, sincere young lady; a talent that knows no bounds. A personality that looms so large, you only need to call her by one name. All this is Brandy.

Brandy was born in McComb, Mississippi, 20 miles north of the Louisiana border, 100 miles from the state capital of Jackson. Her parents, Willie and Sonja Norwood were very religious, raised in the church. Willie was the director of the church choir in Brookhaven, MS; Sonja worked at the local H&R Block office. Their first child, Brandy Norwood, made her first public appearance on February 11, 1979. At the moment of her birth, her mom had a premonition. She knew her daughter was going to grow up to be someone special, a star.

From the moment she could talk, Brandy began to sing. Because her dad led the church choir, Brandy spent lots of time in the choir loft, singing along with the congregation. Many churchgoers remarked about Brandy's amazing voice, and urged Willie to let his baby daughter join the choir. He agreed. Within a few months, the tiny girl was a featured soloist. Those who saw little Brandy performed were amazed by her mature voice and her astounding way of captivating a crowd.

By the time Brandy's little brother, Willie Jr., was born, it was clear that Brandy was more than just a talented child—she was a gifted performer, who needed to be in front of an audience. As her amazing voice developed, it became clear that Willie and Sonja needed to think about what they were going to do with their very special daughter.

Although Brandy's parents had strong ties to their Mississippi home, they wanted to do what was best for their child—and they decided to move to California, the center of the music and entertainment world. Willie found a church he could transfer to in Carson, California, so the family packed up and moved to the West Coast.

Brandy and her kid brother, Willie Jr., started school in Carson, and Brandy immediately got involved in school talent shows. Her mother often took her on open-call auditions, try-outs for small parts in TV shows, movies or commercials.

In 1985, Brandy found her ultimate singing inspiration when she heard Whitney Houston singing the sultry ballad "Saving All My Love For You." Brandy told her mom, "I want to be just like her," and started buying all of Whitney's records, studying them carefully, singing along with them, practicing.

In 1989, Brandy got her first acting role—a tiny one, but a role nonetheless—in the film *Arachnaphobia*. Brandy had three whole lines of dialogue—she was definitely not the thing you remembered after leaving the movie theater—but it was a start. In 1992 she appeared in the film *Demolition Man*, with Wesley Snipes—again, the role was small.

Although she loved acting, even in the smallest of roles, it was singing that really drew her, and she continued to move along the musical path. She appeared on *Showtime At The Apollo*, filmed at the world famous Apollo Theater in Harlem—one of the only acts to ever perform there without a record contract. Then she became a back-up singer for the group Immature—a R&B trop composed of Marques "Batman" Houston, Jerome "Romeo" Jones and Kelton "LDB" Kessee. Brandy appeared on stage with them and backed them up vocally on their album, *On Our Worst Behavior*. "She is the most gifted, wonderful singer I've ever known," Batman recalled to *16* magazine. "We really loved having her with us. She is totally the best, ever!"

In the fall of 1992, Brandy enrolled as a freshman at Hollywood High Performing Arts Center. The students there were all actors, singers, musicians or dancers, and

Brandy loved the atmosphere. It was there, though, that Brandy first tasted the entertainment world's nasty side. When she saw that her teacher never encouraged her to go out for auditions, as she did other students, Brandy asked why. "One day I just went up to her and said, 'Why aren't you sending me out on calls?'" Brandy told *Right On* magazine. "And the teacher said, 'Because you aren't drop-dead gorgeous.' My heart just dropped." Although the remark might have destroyed the confidence of some young girls, it simply made Brandy even more determined to succeed.

By 1993, Brandy had attracted the attention of many record labels, but it was Atlantic Records that finally discovered the budding diva. She was 14 when she signed her record contract. At the same time, Brandy the actress won a role in the ABC comedy sitcom *Thea*, about a widow raising a house full of kids on her own. "When I signed my record contest, it was three months before I got the show *Thea*," Brandy told *Tiger Beat* magazine. "The show was in the way for me, because singing came first. I'd be needed in the studio, but I had to say no, because I was taping the show!" But while timing was definitely not great, the learning experience was, and Brandy was grateful for the opportunity to learn the ins and outs of both sides of the business. "I grew up a lot," she told *SuperTeen* magazine. "I learned the responsibilities of having a job, and I learned to be very focused and disciplined." Brandy was also delighted to hear that she'd be singing on the show—it would be an excellent way to tell the world that this was a multi-talented young lady, ready to take the world by storm.

Thea did not become a huge hit, and it didn't last long. Ironically, when the show ended on February 23, 1994, Brandy was in full album-recording mode, recording the final songs and working in the studio, preparing for the release of her debut single. "I was sad to see *Thea* end, because I thought it was a great show," she told *Right On* magazine. "But I didn't have time to feel emotionally devastated, or anything like that—I was working hard on my album, and that was all I was thinking about."

In September of 1994, Brandy released her first single, "I Wanna Be Down," from her debut album, titled simply, *Brandy*. To promote the single, Brandy appeared on several high-voltage tours, opening for Boyz II Men (where she met longtime boyfriend, Wayna Morris) and Whitney Houston. The single soared to number one on the R&B charts, thrilling Brandy and her family. "I couldn't believe it was all happening," Brandy told *Right On* magazine. "It was something I'd dreamed of and worked for, but when it happened, I was really surprised."

Two months later, in November of 1994, Brandy's self-titled, debut album was released, and it too had soared up the charts. By the beginning of 1995, the album had been certified gold, and by February 11, 1995—Brandy's 16th birthday—it had gone platinum, selling over one million copies.

Although Brandy was tasting success in a big way, she was also working hard to remain an "average" teenager. She was still being tutored every day, excelling in her studies. She got involved with a variety of programs geared to support young people, including Pear Performance, which offered college scholarships to young women. Brandy was becoming a strong role model for girls throughout the country, always encouraging young women to stay in school. But while she accepted the title of "role model," she was quick to point out that she was really just a regular kid herself. "I make mistakes and I'm human," Brandy told *Tiger Beat* magazine. "I have pain just like everybody else."

In January of 1996, Brandy branched out again—returning to television, in a brand new sitcom called *Moesha*. The show was created by Vida Spears and Sara Finney, who had come up with an idea for a very positive sitcom about an African-American family. "At first I thought, what kind of name is Moesha?" Brandy told *Right On* magazine. "After I read the script, I was like, 'This girl is me!'"

And it was Brandy who gave the show it's special

spark. She was determined to keep it real—she really wanted teenagers to connect with Moesha and her hopes, dreams and problems. "I think our show really shows what kids are going through," she told *16* magazine. "It's really fresh, and real—that's really important to me."

And while Brandy was busy getting "fresh and real" on TV, she was also getting nominated—by major award committees! She was nominated for Best Newcomer at the Grammy Awards, although she didn't win; she was also nominated for Best Soul/R&B New Artist at the American Music Awards, and that award she took home. A few months later, she won a Soul Train Award for R&B New Artist. But although she was winning armfuls of awards, it was a prom date that really got her into the news. Brandy accompanied Los Angeles Laker basketball star Kobe Bryant to his Junior Prom at Merion High School, outside of Philadelphia. The pair had met at an awards show (where Brandy was spending most of her time that year). "When I met him, I was like, 'Oh God, you're cute!'" Brandy admitted to *Right On* magazine. "We talked every day before the prom, so we could really get to know each other. I was like, 'I'm not going to a prom with some guy I don't know!' He seemed like such a nice person, so I asked my mom, and my mom talked to his mom.

Of course, the media was all over the beautiful,

photogenic pair, and rumors of a relationship between them started popping up. But there never was a romance, just a cool friendship between two celebrities who were still just getting used to being in the spotlight.

Brandy continued to work on *Moesha*, and she found it both draining and fulfilling. Her schedule was backbreaking, and she often worked 10 plus hours a day, with some of those hours devoted to schoolwork. Brandy was already looking into colleges, flipping through catalogs and considering her educational options—so it was imperative that she keep up her grades, as she was still being tutored every day, excelling in her studies.

With such an intense TV schedule, it was no wonder that Brandy was hesitant about recording a second album. What many of her fans didn't know was that Brandy was totally terrified, and completely overwhelmed at the thought of recording again. "From 1996 to 1997, something happened," Brandy said on the album notes on her second album, *Never Say Never*. "I didn't know until it was time to record that I was afraid to sing. I was comfortable just acting, so it became difficult for me to go into the studio and really produce."

The truth of the matter was that Brandy was nervous about meeting her fans' expectations. Her first album had been so huge and *Moesha* had become such a sucecssful show, it was difficult for Brandy to work on a new album—she constantly worried that it would not be "good enough."

In 1996, Brandy graduated from high school, and enrolled at Pepperdine University, in Malibu California. She decided to major in psychology, and she was looking forward to the new challenges school would bring.

But the challenge of recording again still seemed to frighten her—until she received a call from Whitney Houston, who'd long been Brandy's idol and mentor. Whitney had a starring role in the film *Waiting To Exhale*, and she would contributed a song to the soundtrack, "Exhale (Shoop Shoop)". Whitney had heard about Brandy's admiration, and returned it tenfold—and she wanted Brandy to contribute a song to the soundtrack as well. Brandy couldn't refuse—and her single, "Sittin' Up In My Room," became the biggest hit from the smash-filled soundtrack album. It also won Brandy an award for Best Song at the MTV Movie Awards, beating out Whitney's "Exhale (Shoop Shoop)".

Brandy's second season of *Moesha* was as busy as her first—but if possible, the show had become even more successful—it represented the biggest hit the UPN Network had seen to date. The show had made Brandy a real "multi-media" personality—never before had a seasoned singer moved into a comedy sitcom with such grace and style. Everyone agreed that Brandy was at a high point in her career, and urged her to record her second album. But Brandy herself was still nervous about it. Her family and those closest to her finally convinced her that the time was right to get back to singing. Brandy agreed, but on her own terms—she wanted to be more involved in this recording process, writing her own songs and helping to produce them too. The summer of 1997 looked like the perfect time to begin recording.

But before Brandy could become too involved in the recording process, fate, in the guise of Whitney Houston, stepped in again. Whitney had been developing an idea of a TV special, a remake of Rogers And Hammerstein's version of *Cinderella*. Whitney was curious—would Brandy like the role of Cinderella? Brandy could definitely not say no to an offer like that—it would mean her acting ability and her vocal talents would be seen by millions of people. "I could believe how lucky I was," Brandy told *TV Guide* magazine. "I really am Cinderella, and Whitney Houston is my fairy godmother. I always think of her that way, as someone extra special. We could never just be friends, because I'm too starstruck. I scream every time she calls me."

Cinderella was an extravaganza in the truest sense of the word. The Wonderful World Of Disney special co-starred Whitney, Whoopi Goldberg and Jason Alexander of *Seinfeld* fame, leading an international and inter-racial troup of actors. The show was an unqualified hit, and Brandy won high praise from critics around the country. Unlike *Moesha*, *Cinderella* gave Brandy the opportunity to act and sing—and to sing a style of music that was totally different than her usual R&B groove. "My friends thought I was singing opera," she told *Right On* magazine. "But they all thought it sounded beautiful." Cinderella also gave *Brandy* the chance to shine in gorgeous costumes, and interact with some very famous faces. "I was so nervous every minute I was on the set," she told *TV Guide* magazine. "Everywhere I went, I saw someone famous—and I would just stare, and be starstruck like a little kid."

Moesha was going through it's third season, and Brandy's second album was seriously in the works. The title would be *Never Say Never*, and Atlantic Records, Brandy's record label, was sure it had another smash hit on its hands. In addition to a more mature, and involved Brandy (an artist who would have a whole lot of say this time around), their were also two famous faces who would add their distinct abilities to the record.

The first artist was Mase, who sang a duet with Brandy to the tune "Top Of The World." Of course, one song together, and the whole "world" surmised that the pair were a romantic couple—a rumor both hotly deny.

The second artist was Monica, who sang along with

Brandy on what would be the song of the summer of 1998—"The Boy Is Mine." The song—a sultry, powerful duet between two "rivals," seeking the affection of a philandering boyfriend—was co-written by Brandy, and it soared to the number one spot on the charts. Where the Mase duet inspired rumors of romance, "The Boy Is Mine" inspired rumors of real rivalry between the two teenage divas, and this rumor seemed to be closer to the truth.

Many of the tracts on *Never Say Never* were written or co-written by Brandy, and it was clear that the album was a real statement, a clear picture of Brandy abilities, hopes, dreams and goals for the future. It was Brandy's voice speaking out to her fans, and her future fans—telling them all that this was one diva who was truly here to stay.

Brandy was barely finished with the album when another new opportunity came her way—the opportunity to appear in a major movie, *I Still Know What You Did Last Summer*, which was a sequel to the huge Kevin Williamson hit, *I Know What You Did Last Summer*. The original starred Jennifer Love Hewitt, Sarah Michelle Gellar and Freddie Prinze Jr., and had been the surprise hit of 1997. Since Love's character had survived the first ordeal, it was clear a sequel was in order.

In the sequel, Brandy played a friend of the lead

character, Julie, a character who was working her way through college as a waitress, and who kick-boxed as a hobby (a convenient hobby to have in a horror film). Brandy traveled down to Mexico, where the movie was filmed, and although she wanted to bring her mom down with her for moral support, Sonja was busy, managing the music and acting career of Brandy's younger brother, Willie Jr., now nicknamed Ray-J. "I was kind of glad my mom was busy," she told *Entertainment Weekly* magazine. "She doesn't have to worry about me—I'm a grown up now."

Although Brandy was excited about the prospect, but she was also a bit insecure and nervous about the new adventure. In addition, she was determined to make a name for herself in movies, and she wanted to be appreciated for her acting abilities. As "The Boy Is Mine" sparked rumors of a diva battle-royale between Brandy and Monica, *I Still Know What You Did Last Summer* invited rumors of tiffs between stars Brandy and Love Hewitt. "I think people will always have problems with a woman who is strong and speaks her mind," Brandy told *Entertainment Weekly* magazine. "I know I have talent, and I know I can do anything I put my mind to—maybe some people aren't comfortable with that."

Obviously fans were comfortable with it, because *I Still Know* raked in big bucks at the box office, and

Brandy even brought home an award—a Blockbuster Entertainment Award for Favorite Actress In A Horror Movie.

The word diva once was used to describe the talented sopranos who sang arias in operas. Today, the word diva is used to describe any larger-than-life female singer, any female singer known for tempestuous behavior and equally awesome talent. Brandy had long been referred to as a Diva-In-The-Making; she certainly had a voice that was larger that life. When she appeared on VH1's *Divas Live*, with fellow larger-than-life performers Tina Turner and Cher, Brandy knew she'd made it to the majors. The show was watched by millions, and as usual, Brandy was praised by critics and fans alike.

In 1999, with *Moesha* still going strong (and still ranked as UPN's highest rated show) Brandy jumped into another new TV project, a TV movie called *Double Platinum*, co-starring Diana Ross. In it, Brandy plays the estranged daughter of Diana, who rediscovers her mother's love through their shared passion for music. As usual, the Brandy touch was golden—the show, although critically panned, received excellent ratings. "I couldn't believe I was performing with Diana Ross," Brandy told *TV Guide*. "She's the most amazing star in the world, and I got to worked with her every day, and talk to her about everything. It was unbelievable." It seems no matter how long Brandy's in the business, or how much praise is heaped on her, she'll always remain a starstruck kid when it comes to meeting other celebrities.

Brandy's mass appeal is not hard to understand. A sweet, sincere and grounded girl, who conveys an attitude of enthusiasm and freshness, Brandy has an image that stresses education and commitment to career and personal strength. But underneath it all, she is a determined artist, ready and willing to except the hard work, long hours and grueling demands made on performers. And she has absolutely no fear; although she often speaks about her nervousness and insecurity, neither will stand in her way when there is a new challenge to be met. "If I want to try something new, I just do it," Brandy told *Right On* magazine. "No one has ever tried to keep me from exploring and experimenting as an artist. I know I can do anything I put my mind to, and I know I'll always have my family to support and protect and love me. With them behind me, there's no stopping me."

Alanis performs at the Ariston Theatre in Sanremo, Italy in February, 1999.

Alanis Morissette

IF ALANIS MORISSETTE seems like a tough, serious and intense young woman, it's because she inherited those traits from her mom, Georgia, who escaped an anti-Soviet Union uprising in Hungary in 1956, arriving in Canada to begin a new life.

If Alanis sings of the power of love and loyalty, it's because she learned it from her parents, who met when they were only 12 years old. Nine years later, the sweethearts were married in Ottawa.

This powerful, intellectual, emotional singer made her entrance into the world on June 1, 1974—born 12 minutes after her twin brother, Wade. (The twins followed an older brother, Chad.) Her father, Alan, wanted to give his daughter a feminine version of his own name, and chose Alanis after reading the name in a book about Greece.

Alanis' parents were both educators. Georgia is a schoolteacher, Alan a principal. In 1977, they accepted teaching positions at a Canadian NATO base in Lahr, Germany, and they lived there with their children until

1980. For three years, Alanis had a truly continental education, traveling throughout Holland, Austria, Greece and Switzerland in a camper.

In 1980, the family returned to Ottowa, and normal life resumed. Each of the three Morrissette kids enjoyed performing, recording home videos and created their own dance steps. But while Chad and Wade also developed other interests, Alanis remained dedicated to entertaining. Nothing else seemed to hold any attraction for her. She was completely and totally focused on music.

Her intense love of performing became evident to all when she saw family friends Lindsay and Jacqui Morgan, a folk duo, perform in a hotel lounge. For some young people, the experience might have been boring. For Alanis, it was an awakening. "When I saw the Morgans singing, and being my parents' best friends at the time, I realized singing was something I could do too," Alanis told *The Ottawa Times*. "It was something that real people, people I could see and touch—did for a living."

Alanis began pursuing her ambitions, and her parents did everything they could to help her. The signed her up for the dance lessons she craved; they drove her to the auditions she read about. "They gave me so much freedom," Alanis told *The Ottawa Times*. "They knew, as I did, that this was my destiny—to create and to perform." When Alanis was 11, she won the role of an orphan in a local production of *Annie*, and between the ages of nine and 13, she danced in countless recitals. But singing and music was always the ultimate draw for her. She enjoyed the sensation of performing and singing for people, of drawing them out and making them listen to her. At the same time, Alanis was discovering poetry, and taking her first baby steps into song writing. At that young age, Alanis was already exploring with music, using her incredible imagination to create songs that suited her intense, introverted nature.

In 1984, when Alanis was 10, she mailed a cassette of herself singing to her family's friends, the Morgans. They were shocked when they heard how good it was, and even more surprised when they learned that the little girl had actually written many of the songs herself. Her first song was called "Fate Stay With Me," and Lindsay Morgan helped Alanis record it as a gift for her parents. The song, like others she wrote during these early years, were intense and full of adult emotions. "It was partly creative writing," Alanis told *The Toronto Times*. "It was just like writing a story—a story I hadn't experienced myself."

Lindsay Morgan had connections from his years of professional singing, and he urged Georgia and Alan to let him help Alanis. He helped her record a tape to send to The Foundation To Assist Canadian Talent On Record, an organization which helped artists finance their work.

The group sent her $3,000, which was used to get Alanis started.

Another Ottawa folk singer called The Singing Policeman also became a friend to the young Alanis. A well-known local personality, he brought Alanis out with him to small shows—the pair performed in senior homes, hospitals and community auditoriums, and Alanis grew into a skilled, savvy entertainer.

That local exposure led to her starring role on an offbeat TV show called *You Can't Do That On Television*, a variety show for youngsters. Alanis appeared in skits on the show, and learned a lot about performing for the camera. "The show helped me learn how to be myself in front of a camera and not freeze up," she told a Carleton Production documentary crew. But what the show really taught her was, she didn't want to act—she wanted to sing.

Alanis continued to sng whenever she could; local talent shows and festivals offered plenty of opportunity. She eventually met Stephen Klovan, a former figure skating champion, who became her manager and agent. One of the first jobs he found for Alanins involved her twin brother Wade—they appeared in clothing ads for Dalmy Kids' Clothing. Another helpful mentor was Leslie Howe, who became her first producer.

Alanis' next step toward fame was a patriotic one; she

became known as the "Anthem Girl," singing the Canadian National Anthem, "O Canada" at sporting events throughout Ottawa. She also made an appearance on Star Search, performing the old Osmonds song, "One Bad Apple"—she lost, but kept her positive attitude.

Unlike most performers, who wait to get a record deal before making a video, Alanis took an opposite route—she recorded a video for a song called "I'll Walk Away," and used it as an introduction to record companies. MCA Records took the bait, and Alanis had her record deal—although at the time, she was known simply as Alanis. At the time, Alanis was recording pure pop music—on the side, she was experimenting with alternative sounds with a group called The New York Fries. Alanis knew that the pop sound she was recording was not really her—she felt more in touch with herself when she was singing the poetry she'd written, and experimenting with rockier musical sounds. At the time, she listened to those guiding her career, but she made a promise to herself. "I realized that as I got older, it would be more and more important to listen to my gut, and not to anyone else," she told *The Ottawa Times*. "I had to make the decisions for me."

Alanis recorded two albums—*Alanis* and *Now Is The Time*. The first album was pure dance pop music, the second less so, but Alanis definitely became known as a "dancing queen" in Canada.

The first album was enormously successful, the second less so. "People came to identify me with the music from my first album, which was very peppy dance music," Alanis told *The Toronto Times*. "With the second album, I was writing my own songs, and moving into a new direction. I was less concerned with the approval of others as I wrote it. Of course, maybe people just hated the songs on the second album—which is cool too." Whatever the reason, *Now Is The Time* brought Alanis' pop career to an end. She was a has been at 17, and many thought they had heard the last of her. "I was disappointed," she told *The Toronto Times*. "At that point, I couldn't imagine how the music scene would change."

After all the pop-music craziness that dogged Alanis, she looked forward to spending some time on her own, developing as an artist, and growing up. She moved to Toronto, a huge step for someone who was 19 years old, and had never completely taken care of herself. Where some young women might have been enthusiastic and excited, Alanis felt depressed and lonely. She through herself into her work, writing music. She appeared at music showcases, performing songs she wrote with other Toronto-based artists. "I figured out that living alone would either kill me, or be good for me," she told *The Ottawa Times*. "I learned a lot of hard lessons about being alone."

Alanis worked hard, and spent much of her time collaborating with other performers, but despite the glut of new music she was producing, there was no record company at her disposal, ready and willing to cut a new album. To make ends meet, Alanis nabbed a spot as host of a new Canadian TV show called *Music Works*. The show introduced musicians from Canada, performing in front of a live audience; the stage set resembled a small club, and the audience acted as the club's patrons. Alanis received critical acclaim for her hostly duties—she was professional, articulate, and knew a lot about the music industry. Although she enjoyed her stint on the show, she couldn't shake her dreams of becoming a singer and songwriter—and this time, of doing it her way. Even though she'd just settled into life in Toronto, she decided it was time to make a new move, to Los Angeles. "I knew something big was going to happen to me," she told *The Ottawa Times*. "I felt like I had to keep moving to make it happen." Of course, when she moved to LA, something big did happen; she was robbed at gunpoint within a few months of arriving.

Despite that momentous emotional and financial setback, Alanis was again able to meet talented and creative artists, and her own creativity blossomed. She met Glen Ballard, an amazing musician who'd produced artists like Barbra Streisand and Michael Jackson, and two became songwriting collaborators. The two wrote a mountain of songs together, and Alanis was thrilled with the results. "I'd never met anyone so warm and welcoming," she told *The Ottawa Times*. "Our work was good, and the work environment was beautiful."

Alanis might have continued writing excellent pop music with Glen, but then something happened that literally changed her life. In December of 1994, Alanis began experiencing strange feelings of anxiety, and fainting spells. She would break into convulsive sobs, hysterically crying and screaming. She became overwhelmed by the anxiety attacks that plagued her every day, and she knew she had do something to keep them from taking over her life. "The universe was telling me that if I didn't stop and be still, and start thinking about it and releasing it, it would subtly remind me," she told *The Toronto Times*. "I discovered that I could not control the external world; I have an internal world, and that I can control, but I can't control what happens around me." The discoveries Alanis was making regarding her anxiety attacks also helped her make decisions regarding her career and her future. "I thought fame and the public persona would make me peaceful," she told *The Toronto*

Times. "I realized that was wrong. If I was going to be a songwriter and a performer, it would have to be for myself, not for fame. I had to learn to express my feelings, and my vulnerability in my songs."

Alanis was determined to write about her emotional and psychological experiences—to let the world see her vulnerable side. "I wanted the world to know who I was," she told *Entertainment Weekly*.

Alanis and her collaborator, Glen Ballard, began working furiously on new songs, songs which clearly grew from Alanis' more emotional approach to songwriting. One such song was "You Oughta Know"—those who heard the song in its early stages knew it was going to be very important. "It was a clear example of me being completely honest about how I felt about a breakup of a relationship," she told *Details Magazine*. "When I was writing it, I never thought about what it would be like to perform a song like that every night—it's very painful."

On the strength of her new songs, Alanis was signed to Maverick Records (the record company headed by Madonna). It was there that she recorded *Jagged Little Pill*, the album that would do more than just jumpstart Alanis' music career. It would prove to be a colossal breakthrough in the music business, the best selling album ever recorded by a female artist. Energized by the singles "You Oughta Know," "You Learn" and "Ironic," the album soared to the top of the charts, and won the praise of critics and fans throughout the world. Alanis couldn't believe how successful the album became, although she did try to understand why such a large audience of fans connected with it. "It excited people to see someone being that embarrassingly honest," she told *Details Magazine.* "It validated their seemingly embarrassing emotions. When people experience harsh emotions, society tends to move away from them. So when people heard me, they thought, 'Wow, she's not embarrassed. Maybe I shouldn't be either."

Suddenly, Alanis was everywhere—she was re-living her pop-star days, only this time, she was making music she truly believed in. When she began her year-long tour to support the album, she was truly thrilled to be performing her own, personal songs. And every time she took the stage, she addressed the criticisms that her songs were "angry", a comment that was often appearing in the press. "People tend to want to see me as one-dimension—oh, she's so angry!" Alanis told *Rolling Stone* magazine. "Over time, if you listen to the record in its entirety, you will soon come to realize, I am not solely an angry person."

On February 28, 1996, Alanis took home four Grammy Awards for *Jagged Little Pill:* best album, best rock song, best female rock vocal and best rock album. After beating out some high-powered competition, like Mariah Carey, U2 and Nine Inch Nails, Alanis was every inch the reluctant winner and superstar. "She dedicated her album award to "anyone who has ever written anything, from a very spiritual place."

Two weeks later, Alanis swept the Juno Awards (the Junos are the Canadian Grammys). When she took the stage to accept her five awards, she thanked her home country. "I want to say, most people have their growth in private. But an artist's is in public. I want to thank Canada for accepting that in me. It's a pleasure to do what I do, and communicate to you."

According to *Rolling Stone* magazine, *Jagged Little Pill* sold more than 100,000 copies every week during the period of August 6, 1995 through September 22, 1996. And although Alanis was overjoyed by the love and acceptance she received from her fans, she was totally underwhelmed by the album's financial success; she was far more interested in exploring the personal revelations she was discovering through her songwriting. "I think *Jagged Little Pill* only scratched the surface," she told *Spin* magazine. "I know there are a lot of things I still have repressed, that are dying to come out."

For many artists, a success like *Jagged Little Pill* might seem a hard act to follow, but at this stage of her life, Alanis is clearly more interested in the quality of her work, rather than in the quantity of records she sells. Her second album, *Supposed Former Infatuation Junkie*, did not break any sales records, but the singles "Unsent," "So Pure" and "Joining You" each rose up the charts. More importantly, Alanis has used her success as a way to stretch her creative muscles. She directed and scripted the dialog for the video for "Unsent," and won a Much Music Award for Best Director for her efforts. "You always have to strive and push yourself," she explained in *Rolling Stone* magazine. "You can't just rest on work you've done before. And you can't be afraid to try new things."

One of the new things Alanis is definitely looking forward to is pursuing her education. One of Alanis' favorite subjects is psychology, and she wouldn't mind studying it more. "My education was something I had to put on the back burner," she told *The Toronto Times*. "Obviously, I'll never put something that important on the back burner again.

Another new thing Alanis wanted to try was acting—not the variety show type acting she did as a teen, but real, serious film acting. "I've always been open to exploring that part of myself, and that part of the art world," Alanis told *Rolling Stone* magazine, when she was asked about her interest in acting. "But I'm not into doing it because of what it and bring to me. I'm excited by the idea of devoting myself to something as consuming as acting."

She got her chance to act in the film *Dogma*, which was released in November of 1999. The film co-starred Ben Affleck and Matt Damon, and was directed by Alanis' friend, Kevin Smith. "He's brilliant, a true artist," she told *The Denver Post*. "He asked me to take part in the movie right after I got off the road for *Jagged Little Pill*, but I didn't think I'd be of any value to him, because I was so burnt out. A year later, he'd just finished casting the movie, and there was one role left: a cameo of God. I said I'd love to do it. The film is funny and sweet. "

It was also controversial. Ben Affleck and Matt Damon play angels who've been kicked out of heaven, and the movie was criticized by many people. But Alanis believes the film holds a very spiritual view of the afterlife. "Kevin's belief, as is mine, is that God is us," she told *The Denver Post*. "So in playing my role, I concentrated on simply being real."

In addition to acting in front of the camera, Alanis yearn to work behind the cameras. She's already edited a film of one of her concerts, and she's very interested in editing together the concert footage she's been videotaping since she first went on the road—perhaps to create a feature concert film. "I'd love to do a home video type of film," she told *Rolling Stone* magazine. "It's so interesting to me, to reflect on how I've changed through the years. I hope it would interest the fans—to show them that I'm still real."

And being real is the one quality Alanis brings to all her artistic ventures. She simply can't be anything else.

Selena sings in Corpus Christi, Texas in November, 1994.

Selena

LONG BEFORE RICKY Martin and Jennifer Lopez made it cool to be Latino, there was Selena. In the world of Tejano music, Selena was a popular, beloved superstar—a beautiful rose, an angelic young woman, a girl of the people. At the age of 23, she was viciously murdered by a woman who would profess to be a friend and a fan.

Selena's death devastated her fans, fans who'd followed her since her early years, fans who dressed like her, fell in love with her and longed to be her—but what added to their heartbreak was the fact that young Selena, with her powerful, clear voice and her energetic, enthusiastic attitude, was about to embark on a new career path. The Award-winning entertainer was about to bring her brand of Tejano to the world, recording her first English language album. But that dream was shattered on March 31, 1995, the day Selena lost her life, allegedly at the hands of Yolanda Saldivar, her faithful friend.

Selena came by her musical talents naturally. Her father, Abraham Quintanilla, sang in a group called the

Dinos. The group sang at parties and functions throughout Corpus Christi, Texas. The group sang doo-wop, but their hearts were linked to Tejano music—a blend of Mexican rhythms and language, and Anglo, or America influences like rock 'n roll and big band.

Abraham saw music as his way out of poverty, but he encountered tremendous prejudice along the way. White audiences were not interested in seeing a band of Mexican musicians; Mexican natives were troubled by the fact that the group sang American songs. The band disbanded, and Abraham moved with his wife Marcella to Lake Jackson, Texas, where he took a position as a shipping clerk at Dow Chemical.

In 1971, Marcella gave birth to a daughter, a happy addition to a family that included older siblings Isaac, Eddie, Hector, Yolanda, Gloria and Cynthia.

From the beginning, it was clear Selena was a special child. She was beautiful, vibrant, friendly and always smiling. One day when she was still very young, she saw her father playing guitar (he was still passionate about music, and insisted that his older children learn instruments) and she opened up and sang along with him.

Years later, Selena would remark that her reasons for singing at such a young age were actually quite selfish—she saw the attention her father gave to her older siblings' musical instruction, and she wanted some of that attention for herself. "I guess I got a little jealous," she was quoted as saying. "When my father saw that I was interested in singing, he started teaching me, and I guess he noticed that I picked it up right away. My father would make us all sing for our family." Despite bouts of shyness, Selena learned to enjoy the attention and admiration of her family. They recognized that she was gifted, and they encouraged her every step of the way.

Abraham was thrilled with her daughter's talent. In her, he saw a way to redirect his musical passions. "When I realized Selena could sing, I saw the continuation of my dream," he was quoted as saying.

Abraham began the difficult and grueling work of training his young daughter for a career in show business. He nurtured and cultivated her talent. Although Selena had lot of friends in school and was, in fact, one of the most popular girls in her class, she was often isolated from them, spending hours alone with her father, always practicing. When she wasn't working, she was listening to music: her favorites were disco queen Donna Summer, the pop group Air Supply and the female vocal group A Taste Of Honey.

In the summer of 1980, when Selena was only nine, her father decided to create a family singing group, using all his children—although it was clear that Selena was truly the main attraction. The family performed at Papa

Gayo's restaurant in Lake Jackson, Texas, and Selena was soon spotted by Freeport, TX radio station KBRZ. Disc jockey Primo Ledesma played a tape of the youngster on his show, and within seconds, listeners began calling in to ask, "Who is the little girl with the big voice?"

Abraham continued steering his family towards music; as a family, they performed at weddings, country clubs and local eateries. The group specialized in *musica tejana*, a quirky combination of Spanish lyrics and danceable melodies. But Abraham also nurtured his daughter's talents. He entered her in local talent shows, which she usually won, singing her version of the ultra-sentimental hit song, "Feelings."

Although her family was constantly on the move, and she herself was constantly performing, young Selena still excelled in school. She was exceptionally bright and eager to please, but her teachers still worried about her absences and her late hours singing and rehearsing.

Eventually, the family moved back to Corpus Christi. Abraham believed the move would benefit Selena's musical career. "We really starting working hard on our music when we returned to Corpus Christi," Selena remembered. "We had no other alternative; we had to make money."

Abraham encouraged Selena to record songs at Hacienda Studios in Corpus Christi, and although she put in a professional performance, her recordings went nowhere. The family, playing under the name Los Dinos, worked steadily, although there were often family arguments about what music to play. The Quintanilla kids, including Selena, loved Top 40 music, and wanted to pursue a more American sound. Their father was adamant that they perform only in Tejano, which was a much more bankable form of music in Corpus Christi. Selena, who was the group's lead singer, perfected her Spanish; no one who heard her sing ever knew that she could barely speak Spanish. The family consistently got work throughout the area; and Abraham was always happy to play the guitar, or sing a duet with his young daughter whenever neccessary. "We all wanted to make it, so we did whatever we could," Selena said about those tough, early years. "We sometimes played to an audience of 10 people, but we always put on the best show we could—we knew we had to give our all, no matter what."

The group made a few records under the name Selena y los Dinos—and with their constant touring, the group became well known throughout South Texas. Selena's awesome voice caught everyone's attention. Abraham kept the family's name in the spotlight, pushing the band to perform whenever possible. "It was really frustrating sometimes," Selena was quoted as saying. "At times, we all felt, let's give it up. Let's everyone get real jobs. But something held us to the music."

By the time Selena turned 15, she was a minor celebrity in South Texas. She appeared twice on the cover of Tejano Entertainer Magazine. Inside, the magazine article praised her for "making an impressive contribution to the Hispanic music industry as the youngest female vocalist in the Tejano music circuit today." The group released three consecutive singles that received considerable airplay—the song "Dame un Beso" was her first serious hit; the single "A Million To One," her first number one in Texas.

In 1987, Selena won the first of her many Tejano Music Awards—she took home the coveted Female Entertainer Of The Year Award, and was amazingly modest when she said, "God, that's neat! At least I know I'm accomplishing something." That year, she and the group released an album called "And The Winner Is," to commemorate all the awards Selena was bringing home. The title may have sounded arrogant, but anyone who knew Selena knew that she was unfazed by her rapidly soaring success. "I guess we're really addicted to the public," she said of her group—and of herself. "I only think of the shows as our way of showing people a good time. It's all for them."

In 1987, Selena and her family also discovered Gloria Estefan, who had broken into the mainstream with her single "The Conga." Abraham began to realize that Selena also belonged in the "mainstream"—that her talent knew no bounds. But the traveling and touring were already taking a toll on Selena, who was, by the age of 16, a bona fide star of the Tejano music circuit, a well-known role model and celebrity to thousands of citizens throughout the Southwest. "I miss going to school and having friends," she confided to reporters. "I miss being around kids my own age, and I had a very boring childhood because I never had the opportunity to associate without anyone my own age, due to my career. I always took my career seriously—when you go out on the road and make a profession of it, you always wonder if people are going to accept you—that's why you always have to take it seriously."

Although Selena was already a seasoned professional at 16, she often dreamt of following her own dreams, for though she loved music, it was clear that her father was the one who really wanted to pursue it as a full-time career. "I've been designing clothes for a while," Selena mused. "One day I might try opening a boutique, although I truly try not to think that far ahead."

When she was 18, Selena got a serious record deal with Capitol-EMI Latin, which was looking to expand into the Latin market "discovered" by Gloria Estefan. In other words, now that one artist was successful, record companies were looking to find "copies." Selena recognized that the success of Gloria Estefan had opened doors for her, and was quoted as saying, "I feel very fortunate, because I was at the right place at the right time." But if Capitol EMI was looking for a carbon-copy, they soon realized that what they'd actually found was a remarkable, unique performer—everyone knew Selena had limitless potential. She was beautiful, smart, a complete professional on stage, and she had a vocal range that overwhelmed even jaded record company producers.

In 1989, Selena y los Dinos were working on their first Capitol album, called simply, *Selena*. The music they recorded was a blending of Tex-Mex and Latin Pop. The general consensus was that Selena could sing anything, English or Spanish. Meanwhile, Selena was endorsing Coca-Cola, which was sponsoring much of her touring activity. With the endorsements, and the success of her album, Selena was easily a millionaire by her 19th birthday. More importantly, she was an important role model for the Hispanic community, representing a new, independent woman who could build a strong career and still be remarkably feminine and family-centered. Her image was so revered, she was chosen as a spokesperson for the Texas Prevention Partnership, sponsored by the Texas Commission on Alcohol and Drug Abuse. Her message was straightforward and strong: "With a positive attitude, you can be anything you want to be."

In 1991, the band expanded, bringing in a shy guitar player named Chris Perez. He was two years older than Selena, but like her, he was a seasoned professional on stage, and his playing gave the group a rockier, harder edge. Selena found herself captivated by him. "I never thought I would marry a musician," she confided to friends. But on April 2, 1992, that's exactly what she did. She was 21 years old. Although she dreamed of a huge wedding and a formal white dress, Selena and her groom celebrated their wedding at a justice of the peace's office, both wearing jeans. Although her father approved of the match, he urged the young newlyweds to keep news of their marriage quiet—he felt the fans would not be as accepting as he was.

In 1992, Selena released the album Entre a Mi Mundo, which soared to the top of the Latin and Mexican-regional charts. Selena-fever was now spreading to Mexico—a country which usually favored performers who had blonde hair and blue eyes. The people of Mexico flocked to embrace Selena, declaring her "una artista del pueblo," an artist of the people, and almost overnight, she was the Tejano star of Mexico.

Selena continued to make plans regarding her English language album, and she was determined to stay true to her style while moving into the mainstream. "It'll be my style, definitely," she was quoted as saying. "I know that with this Spanish international and English thing, it's just like starting all over again, but we have the experience. I just know I have to stay true to what I've been doing."

Part of that style meant having a say in everything that went on in her professional life. Although her brother A.B. ran the production and publishing companies, and her sister Suzette handled merchandising (ordering, printing and selling the t-shirts, caps and other items with Selena's smiling face on them), it was Selena who controlled her own image. "I'm in charge of all the outfits and costumes," she said. "I design clothing and jewelry on the side—I love shiny things, and I love clothing. Someday I'll have my own business, and I'll have a mail-order catalogue coming out soon. So everyone can buy my belts and all that junk!"

It was at this time, during all the excitement and the promise of a career that would span the globe, that Selena met Yolanda Saldivar, a resident of San Antonio, Texas. Yolanda was tiny, less than five feet tall, and Selena called her "Buffy." She was eleven years older than Selena, had been working as a nurse, and she had never been a fan of Tejano music, but when she saw the younger woman perform, she became devoted. She arranged to meet Selena's father Abraham, and convinced him to allow her to start a fan club in 1991. She was dedicated and determined, and within four years, Yolanda had built a fan club membership of almost five thousand people. She gave up her nursing career to work full-time for Selena and her family.

Because Selena was so busy, she needed someone like Yolanda to lean on. Selena was pursuing her apparel design business with the same dedication she'd give to music, and plans had already been drawn up for a string of boutiques. Yolanda got involved with that end of the business to, helping Selena as she built her dream.

Selena was now performing in 60,000 seat arenas all over the Southwest, and her latest album, *Selena Live*, was a huge hit. But on January 27, 1994, Selena's real dream came true—her boutique, Selena Etc., opened in Corpus Christi. Selena was delighted. "I want to do something outside the music business," she said modestly; but her heart was jumping as she gazed at her first boutique. She and fashion designer Martin Gomez created a shop that presented Selena's fashion personality. Although Selena would have been perfectly happy working in the boutique and making clothes, she had too many professional touring and recording duties to think about. She turned some of the responsibilities of running the boutique over to her good friend, Yolanda Saldivar. It wasn't long before Yolanda was officially manager of the shops in Corpus Christi, as well as shops opening in San

Antonio and other Texas locations. Although Selena trusted Yolanda, Selena's partner Martin Gomez thought otherwise. He neither trusted nor liked Yolanda, and he considered her a nuisance and an incompetent.

Selena was enjoying the fruits of her constant labors, and she put all the money she made into the stores. She really believed that it was important to start up small businesses and provide jobs for the people she sang for. She always reveled in her free time, at home with her husband Chris. "For me, the ideal day is when I'm in jeans around my house," she was quoted as saying. "I like to clean my house—I mop the floor, clean the walls, wash the car and the dog, I make my bed, I even cook sometimes, although I admit I'm not that good. That's why they invented pizza home delivery. Fortunately I have a husband who isn't at all macho, and who helps me with the household chores."

Selena's next Spanish language album, *Amor Prohibido*, was a real victory for her. The album climbed to the number one position of the Latin charts, where it remained (dipping occasionally to number two) for most of 1994. *Texas Monthly* magazine declared her one of the twenty most important Texans of 1994. She was sitting on top of the world—and ready to take it over in a big way.

But already, some clouds were floating over Selena's

bright world. The first was Yolanda, the steadfast fan and friend who was running the boutiques. There were signs of financial mismanagement, and Yolanda was being blamed. Other employees disliked Yolanda's personality, and her devotion to Selena was seen by others as obsession. Another cloud was floating over her marriage. Selena had met a cultured, refined and very sophisticated man, a plastic surgeon named Ricardo Martinez, and although the two were just friends, it was clear Selena's relationship with her husband Chris was under a considerable strain. Finally, there were problems with her always overly protective father, who controlled much of Selena's money, and seemed to be determined to use it to control her.

Still, Selena continued to press forward with her boutiques, devoting as much time to them as to her music career. She sought our perfumers to create a fragrance that would bear her name. She was determined to build her fashion business with her own two hands. Her father had led her to music, but fashion was her world, and she was proud of her success there. But even that happiness was short-lived. The shops didn't make a lot of money, and before long, store employees were being laid off. Once again, Yolanda was blamed—but only behind the scenes. No one had the heart to accuse Selena's friend of cheating her, with only suspicions and no real proof.

Selena's father, Abraham, had no such reservations. When her heard that Yolanda was suspected of bad behavior towards his daughter, he was infuriated. He accused her of cheating his daughter, and of being a liar and thief. He told her to stay out of Selena's life. Selena was heartbroken to lose such a trusted friend, and upset that she'd believed so strongly in Yolanda.

But Selena could only concentrate on the lost friendship for so long—she had to focus on her crossover album, the one that was going to bring her the worldwide audience she craved. One of the songs she was working on was called "Dreaming Of You," and she thought it had all the makings of a huge hit. She was looking forward to introducing her music to a whole new audience. "I want the very best that America has to offer and the best of what the Hispanic world has to offer," she was quoted as saying.

On March 31, 1995, Selena was truly in an enviable position; to the world outside, looking in at her, she had the world at her feet. The film *Don Juan de Marco* was opening, and Selena had a small cameo role in it. She was scheduled to headline two major arena tours in May, and she was working hard, selecting songs for her English language album. But the Yolanda problem was still bothering her; it was becoming clearer that Yolanda had been taking advantage of Selena's love and trust, scamming money from the boutique business. But Yolanda had also told Selena that she'd been assaulted by a stranger, and needed Selena's help. Selena couldn't just turn her back on the woman she once thought was her closest friend.

Selena went to Doctors Regional Medical Center to check up on Yolanda, but the nurses on duty told her that Yolanda's assault story had been a hoax. Angry at being used again, Selena stormed over to the motel room Yolanda was staying in and accused her face to face of betrayal. After a heated exchange, Yolanda allegedly pulled out a gun and shot Selena in the right shoulder. Selena ran from the motel room, to the entrance of the motel, where she collapsed in a pool of blood. By the time she was taken to the hospital, she was gone. The cause of death was internal bleeding and cardiac arrest.

The news stunned the Tejano musical community. Grieving fans were inconsolable, calling radio stations and crying hysterically, declaring their love for their goddess with poems and love songs. They held vigils outside Selena's boutiques, holding candles and placing bouquets of flowers at the door.

Meanwhile, Abraham, who was also inconsolable, held a press conference to announce that Selena had intended to fire Yolanda, and that that provided the motive for the shooting. Yolanda refused to turn herself in to police, instead holing up in a truck for 10 hours in a massive police standoff. When she finally did turn herself in, she gave a statement which blamed everything on Selena's father, saying her had planted the seeds of distrust in Selena. She refused to accept responsibility for the shooting.

In death, ironically, Selena achieved the worldwide fame she sought throughout her life. Around the United States, newspapers and TV stations told the story of the beautiful, talented, happily married and universally beloved Tejano singer whose life was so tragically cut down. She became a symbol of promise—everyone who had known her was certain that mainstream success was just an album away.

Selena's life and death received even more publicity when disc jockey Howard Stern belittled Selena and her fans, saying "Spanish people have the worst taste in music," and suggesting that Selena's fame had come only because of the grisly manner of her death.

Although the remarks were cruel and crude, they also held a grain of truth—to most of the United States, Selena was an unknown. People in New York, California, Iowa and Oregon never heard of the sensual siren with the voice of an angel. But to the Southwestern Tejano community, and especially to Texas, Selena was an icon of shining womanhood, a role model who possessed the zest for life, the talent and the love of the people in abundance. To them, her loss could never be measured. Selena's fans revere her in death; the number of Web pages devoted to Selena continues to grow. She remains a part of their world and their culture. She remains, as always, Selena, artist of the people.

Although Yolanda is currently serving a sentence of life in prison for the slaying of Selena, she maintains to this day that there is "another story" regarding the crime. She claims that she loved Selena like a daughter, and that the motive for the violence was Selena's diary, which Yolanda had possession of, and which revealed Selena's innermost thoughts, thoughts Selena did not want revealed. Yolanda insists that when she reveals her entire story, she'll be set free—but that "true story" has not yet been told.

Since Selena's death, the Latin music market has exploded with artists like Ricky Martin, Jennifer Lopez and the Iglesias brothers, Enrique and Julio, leading the way. Today, mainstream Latin pop music is heard on every radio across the country, celebrated on MTV with sultry music videos, and played in dance clubs where thousands of fans dance to the infectious rhythms. One could only imagine the heights Selena could have climbed to had she been given the chance. There is no doubt that with her talent, drive, enthusiasm and winning personality, she would have been a sensation.

LeAnn Rimes performs at the Country Music Association Awards Show in Nashville in September of 1997.

LeAnn Rimes

SHE HAS BEEN called the second coming of Patsy Cline, a little girl with a big, big voice. She has been credited with re-energizing country music, paying homage to its traditional roots, yet she's achieved phenomenal crossover success. Seventeen-year-old LeAnn Rimes is already a music legend.

She was born, as so many country music legends are, in a small town—Jackson, Mississippi. Her parents, Wilbur and Belinda, considered her a small miracle—they had been told at the start of their marriage that children would not be possible. Although they had a happy life—Wilbur sold equipment for an oil company and Belinda was a receptionist—they longed for a baby, and Belinda soon turned to prayer. God's answer was LeAnn, and her parents were devoted to her.

From the moment she was born, the Rimes knew their only daughter was destined for great things. She was an independent, excitable child who filled every childhood second with tap dance lessons, baseball and gymnastics.

But singing was her passion from the word go; by the time she was two, she was singing along with her mother's lullabies. Wilbur was an amateur guitar player, and he encouraged his daughter to sing along with his plinking version of "You Are My Sunshine." "I was always encouraged to sing," LeAnn told *Modern Screen's Country Music*. "It was a part of my life since I was born, and I always knew it was important to me."

At an early age, LeAnn was influenced by broadway show tunes and artists like Barbara Streisand and Judy Garland. She had already learned how to place her parents' records on the stereo turntable, and her parents were astounded at her abilities. "I could sing better than I could talk," LeAnn told *Country Weekly*.

It was not long before friends and neighbors began to encourage Wilbur and Belinda to get LeAnn into show business, but her parents were hesitant about letting their tiny daughter perform in public. When a dance teacher urged Belinda to get LeAnn involved in local talent competitions, she balked. But soon, both her parents realized that LeAnn wanted to sing more than anything else in the world. In 1988, when she was just six, they entered her in a local talent show—she sang "Getting To Know You," from *The King And I*. Wilbur, who was certain she wouldn't win (and couldn't bear to see LeAnn disappointed), had decided to go on a hunting trip that

day, and when he returned, he was astonished to see
LeAnn clutching the trophy she'd won. "He started
crying," LeAnn recalled to *Country Weekly*. "He just
couldn't believe I'd won the whole thing."

Although critics have suggested that her parents
pushed her into show business, the truth was, LeAnn was
the one doing the pushing. "I know all little kids have
dreams of what they want to do when they grow up,"
LeAnn told *Country Weekly*. "Mine never changed. I told
my parents what I wanted, and they just kind of helped me
along. I've kind of pushed my parents more than they
pushed me."

The first big push was out—of Mississippi, that is.
Since there weren't local avenues for LeAnn to pursue
her singing dreams, her parents agreed to move to Texas,
where there were more opportunities for young
performers. They moved to a two-bedroom apartment in
Garland, Texas. Wilbur and Belinda's nervousness about
letting LeAnn perform at such a young age evaporated
when they realized how truly special her abilities were. "I
wanted to accomplish my dream of being something," she
told *Modern Screen's Country Music*. "I wanted to start
early."

And start early she did. Her official Dallas, Texas
debut was appearing on a float in a local pageant. People
were blown away by the powerful voice coming from the

tiny little girl, and it wasn't long before she was appearing on local shows, then moving to a series of "Little Opry" stages throughout Dallas and Forth Worth. "I'd sleep in the car," LeAnn recalled to *Modern Screen's Country Music.* "We'd get to the stage, and I'd get up there and sing, 'Crazy' by Patsy Cline, which was my favorite song." Wilbur and Belinda were now full-time, "manager parents," driving LeAnn from show to show, taking care of her, and encouraging her along the way. They were so confident that LeAnn's talent could conquer the world, that they decided to bring her to New York City, so she could try out for the lead role in the Broadway show, *Annie II.*

It would prove to be one of LeAnn's few professional disappointments. The producers of *Annie II* thought LeAnn was too young to carry the show, and they were concerned that her Southern accent would be inappropriate for the show. "It was difficult to lose that role," LeAnn told *Country Weekly.* "But I think I learned a lot about rejection at a younger age than other kids who get into this business—and you have to deal with rejection." To lift LeAnn's spirits, her parents bought her a dog named Sandy, which was the name of dog in *Annie II.*

The following year, when she was seven years old, LeAnn made her stage debut as Tiny Tim in a Dallas musical production of *A Christmas Carol.* She received rave reviews and loud applause from appreciative audience, but while she appeared to have a natural ability for acting, her true love was still music. She continued to sing whenever she could, while maintaining an A average in school.

That year also brought LeAnn to the Johnnie High Country Music Revue, which featured local musicians and celebrities. Audience came from all Texas to hear little LeAnn, dressed in her frilly white dresses, belting out country classics. "It was great training for me," she told *Modern Screen's Country Music.* "I learned the importance of being professional. It was hard work."

In 1990, LeAnn appeared on the national TV talent show, *Star Search.* She sang "Don't Worry About Me," and was a two-week champion. "It was my first time on national TV," she told *Country Weekly.* "I didn't look nervous, but of course I was, a little."

A local celeb after *Star Search,* LeAnn was more sought after than ever. She sang the National Anthem a cappella at Dallas Cowboys football games, the Walt Garrson Rodeo and The National Cutting Horse Championship in Fort Worth. It was inevitable that she be "discovered" along the way—and she was. A Fort Worth disc jockey and composer named Bill Mack noticed LeAnn, and was moved by her voice and talent.

Why was Bill Mack such an important man in LeAnn's life? Because years ago, Bill Mack had written a song called "Blue," which he'd given to Patsy Cline to record. When she died in a fiery plane crash in 1963, Bill gave up his dream of having the song recorded, since he believed in his heart that it was "Patsy's song." But when he heard LeAnn, his dream came back to life. Wilbur, who was looking for songs for his daughter to record, met with Bill, but he almost said no to "Blue," thinking the lyrics were too old for his daughter. But LeAnn thought differently. "I knew 'Blue' was perfect for me," she told *Country Weekly.* "I kept bugging my dad about it. When he played the tape for me, I added the little yodel thing to the 'blue' line, and my dad said, "OK, now we have to record it."

In 1993, when LeAnn was 11, she began working on her first album, which would include a recording of "Blue." Although she was delighted with her professional accomplishments, there were some problems on the home front—namely, school. Although she was an excellent student, she was having a hard time because of her local celebrity status. "I was threatened a lot," she told *Modern Screen's Country Music.* "I had a rough time. Kids thought I was different from everybody else, which I'm not. I cried because I couldn't understand why they thought I was different. " Belinda decided to take LeAnn out of school, and found her a home tutor. LeAnn was thrilled—she was able to concentrate on her schoolwork again, and she soared back up to her usual A average.

When she was not studying, she was in the studio with her father, who was producing the album. Her first CD was called *All That,* and it was sold at LeAnn's local shows. Eventually the Blockbuster Music chain became interested in carrying it. Suddenly, the little album was everywhere! And of course, Nashville, the country music capital, was soon knocking on LeAnn's door.

For two years, LeAnn made the rounds in Nashville, auditioning for a variety of record companies. Wilbur, acting as her manager, said no to many offers; he just didn't feel they were right for LeAnn. Eventually, she was signed by Curb Records. Wilbur was happy that the deal would allow him to continue managing LeAnn. "We would be able to have a little control that way," LeAnn explained to *Billboard* magazine.

Between 1995 and 1996, LeAnn kept busy in the studio. She re-recorded "Blue" for the new album—that single would provide the title for the record. She even wrote a few songs, including "Talk To Me," which was also included on the album. And she recorded a song called "Cattle Call" with legendary singer Eddie Arnold. Curb released a copy of "Blue" to disc jockeys, and before long, it was clear that the song was creating a sensation. "I think a lot of country music fans who are younger don't know what the older, traditional country sounds like," LeAnn told *Billboard* magazine. "It's wonderful that they're liking "Blue,' because it reflects where country music started. It's true country music. It stood out from everything else being played on the radio."

The album was released on July 9, 1996, and it blew to the top of the country charts. LeAnn immediately broke a record; she was the youngest country singer to ever have a debut album hit the top slot in the first week of release. In Nashville, the music scene was buzzing, but LeAnn was on the road, hundreds of miles away from the craziness. "I couldn't believe it debuted at number one," LeAnn told *Country Weekly.* "It's humbling that my album may make country history. It's humbling and cool."

What really blew Nashville away was that LeAnn's album was also at the top of the pop charts—it would get as high as number three, behind heavy metal rockers Metallica. "It's exciting and amazing," LeAnn told *Billboard* Magazine. "I can't believe it, it really is an achievement for me."

The album's second single, "One Way Ticket (Because I Can)" was another number one success, on all the *Billboard* charts, another one for the record books. But as success brought LeAnn into the public eye, so came the controversies. The first: a tabloid reported that LeAnn was not 13 years old, but was actually only ten. LeAnn and her parents had to go on TV with an enlargement of her birth certificate to prove her age. Then came the criticism that LeAnn shouldn't be recording love songs that made her sound more "experienced" than she actually was. "I don't think I have to experience anything in order to sing these songs," she said on *Entertainment Tonight.* "I can basically feel these songs. I've seen people get hurt before—my close friends have gotten hurt, and I know what they're going through. I'm not going to sing little kid songs about getting out of high school. I'm trying to appeal to everyone, from eight to 80."

The controversy didn't slow down sales of her album—on her 14th birthday, LeAnn received a Gold Record for *Blue.* LeAnn was now a young teenager in demand. She traveled the country, performing at fairs and festivals, and she appeared at star-studded events in Nashville. She met her idols, Reba McEntire and Vince Gill, plus superstars like Trisha Yearwood and Wynonna. She appeared on The Late Show With David Letterman, and was thrilled to appear on the New York City stage. But most importantly, she met with her legion of fans; her mother, Belinda, was in charge of her ever-growing fan club. "It's so cool to have fans," she told *Country Weekly.*

"It's fantastic to know there are so many people out there, who you don't know, who are supporting you."

Her concerts became the hottest tickets in town. Everyone wanted to catch a glimpse of her, and to hear her amazing voice. LeAnn felt absolutely no nervousness when she stepped on stage to perform; it was as if she was born to be on stage. "There's nothing to compare to how I feel when I'm on stage," she told *Modern Screen's Country Music*. "I love getting up there and seeing the fans. It's neat to see them singing my songs." In addition to her hit songs, LeAnn speckled her concerts with tons of familiar favorites, like "Crazy" and "Stand By Me."

In late 1996-1997, the awards began to rush in: an American Music Award, followed by two Grammys, including Best New Artist. (Again, LeAnn broke ground—she was the first country artist to take home that particular award). She also won three Academy of Country Music Awards, a TNN Music City News Award and the Horizon Award from the Country Music Association. She closed 1997 with four Billboard Music Awards, including Artist of the Year. "Winning awards is definitely exciting," LeAnn told *Billboard* Magazine. It's a sign that people like you and respect you. But I'd continue to sing, even if I never won any awards."

LeAnn's two subsequent albums, *Unchained Melody, LeAnn The Early Years* and *You Light Up My Life:*

Inspirational Songs, were also extremely successful. The former sold multi-platinum, and the latter topped three music charts, pop, country and Contemporary Christian. But it was the end of 1997 that brought LeAnn her greatest successes, and yet another controversy.

LeAnn's grandmother had passed away while she was traveling in Nashville, and she was unable to say goodbye to her—that simple, sad story led to the book *Holiday In Your Heart.* LeAnn joined forces with Tom Carter, a well-known Nashville-based author, and helped to create the story of Anna Lee, a teenage country singer. Anna is on her way to sing at The Grand Opry, when her beloved grandma gets sick. Although her grandmother urges her to come home, Ann decides to stick around Nashville to jump start her career. Of course, her priorities are turned around when she meets a mysterious old woman known only as "The Legend," who leads Anna through a loving journey that proves to her that only family can bring a "holiday to your heart." "It was my story," she told *Country Weekly.* "Tom wrote down my ideas, and the book just came out."

Of course, the success of the book made it a natural for a Christmas movie, and in December of 1997, it aired on ABC—starring LeAnn herself as Anna! "The book's character is a singer, and the movie included my music," she told *Teen Country* Magazine. "I'm interested in acting, and in this movie, I get to act and sing, which was very exciting."

LeAnn co-starred with Bernadette Peters in the film, and she did a respectable job in her first acting outing, although some critics took great joy in insulting her abilities. LeAnn was quick to tell her fans that she wasn't interested in leaving singing for acting in movies.

And it was the movies that brought her controversy in 1997. That year, a film called *Con Air* was released, and LeAnn was originally scheduled to sing the movie's theme song, the beautiful ballad "How Do I Live." When the producer's heard her version, they weren't completely happy with the sound, and they called in country superstar Trisha Yearwood to re-record it. That was the version that would eventually be heard in *Con Air*.

LeAnn, and everyone else involved with her musical career, was not amused—LeAnn released her version of "How Do I Live" to pop radio, while Trisha's version climbed the country radio charts. For much of 1997, the songs dueled; savvy music types even spliced together the versions, so both could be heard at once. The situation made LeAnn a bit uncomfortable. "From my success, I learned that I'm not the only one in the world who can be successful," she told *Teen Country* Magazine. "Everybody has a talent, and a lot of people are good at things I'm not. I think I've learned not to get a big head, because I'm not better than anyone else. Things happen for a reason. And this success must have a reason for me. But I think it can happen to anyone, if you work really hard for it."

In 1998, LeAnn released *Sittin' On Top Of The World*. The CD featured the hit single "Commitment," as well as the lovely ballad "Looking Through Your Eyes," which was heard in the Disney animated movie, "Quest For Camelot." LeAnn also embarked on a monster tour with country heartthrob Bryan White—the two set off across the country on their "Something To Talk About" Tour. (Rumors of course flew when the pair got together on stage to sing together; the truth was that while LeAnn may have harbored a crush on Bryan, who was eight years her senior, he was dating actress Erica Paige). It was clear that Bryan was thrilled to be working with the powerhouse singer. "I think people should take a little time to respect LeAnn's talent," he told *Teen Country* Magazine. "We love singing together. We have such a mutual respect for each other and far as our music is concerned—we're tickled to be working together,"

Despite all the touring, all the recording, and all the constant work, LeAnn remained a totally typical teenager. Shopping was and is a passion, and she's really into softball and horseback riding. "I'm really pretty average," she told *Country Weekly* Magazine. "A lot of people may think I missed out on a lot of things like school, but the truth is, I prefer being tutored, because I can really concentrate on my studies." Of course, she acknowledges that her environment is a little unusual. "A lot of my friends are between 20 and 80 years old," she told *Country Weekly*. "My closest friends are the members of my band. "

Unfortunately, in 1998, LeAnn experienced something a lot of teenagers face: the separation of her parents. Belinda and Wilbur divorced, and although they both still remain close to LeAnn, the shock of the split upset LeAnn greatly. LeAnn also began to spend more and more time in California, where she continued to pursue her acting dreams. And she couldn't help but be disappointed when *Sittin' On Top Of The World* failed to make it to the top of the charts, as her previous albums had.

In 1999, LeAnn released her album, simply titled, *LeAnn Rimes*. The album was devoted to traditional country music, with remakes of such classic songs as 'Your Cheatin' Heart" and "Me And Bobby McGee." The first single, "Big Deal," was written by country songwriters Al Anderson and Jeffrey Steele. LeAnn was thrilled to celebrate her country roots. "I really feel connected to this music," she told *Country Weekly*. "It's the sound I grew up with, and the sound I feel more comfortable with. Even though I've had some success on the pop charts, I'll never abandon my country roots. I couldn't."

But 1999 was more than just a year of tradition. It was a year of new, and exciting endeavors for the 17-year old LeAnn. She performed "Written In The Wind," a duet with Elton John from his album *Aida* on The People's Choice Awards, and also made an appearance on *VH1's Diva's Live.* "Part of this business involves meeting famous people," LeAnn told *People* Magazine. "Still, meeting Sir Elton John was one of the greatest experiences in my life."

LeAnn's acting career is also heating up. She appeared on *Moesha,* the sitcom that stars R&B/Pop superstar Brandy, another young singer who knows how tough life in the spotlight can be. "She was great fun to talk to," LeAnn told *People* Magazine. 'We share a lot in common."

The talented, stylish and intelligent LeAnn is a young woman in demand—she served as *Good Morning America's* celebrity host for the American Music Awards and she appeared on *The Today Show's* summer concert series. She's often seen on the arm of handsome actor Andrew Keegan (*10 Things I Hate About You* and *O*). And of course, she graduated high school. "I take everything one day at a time," she told *Country Weekly*

Magazine. "I'm hoping my career lasts a long time, I want to continue acting and singing and writing songs. And I'd love to give college a try. That's definitely an option for me. I've always wanted to help children, and I've thought about studying speech pathology."

Of course the future is wide open for LeAnn, but music will always be a part of her life. "Music is my dream come true," LeAnn told *Teen Country* Magazine. "I would never turn my back on my dream."

Go, Girl!

Mariah Carey perform during the Nobel Peace Prize Concert in
Oslo's National Theatre in December of 1997.

Mariah Carey

MARIAH CAREY HAS been pop music's ultimate diva for over a decade, and this charismatic, fiery, talented and temperamental singer shows no signs of slowing down. This amazing performer, a seemingly overnight sensation, can purr a sexy R&B tune with ease, then belt out a ballad and bring a tear to every eye in the audience. There's no doubt that marvelous Mariah has star quality.

But life hasn't always been easy for Mariah. Growing up in a bi-racial family, she quickly learned that in the eyes of others, she was viewed as an outsider. Music was Mariah's salvation; it gave her a way to fit in and the power to bring joy to millions of people around the world.

Mariah's mother, Patricia, was a talented singer in her own right, who traveled from her home to New York City, where she earned a place in the New York City Opera. In 1960, she married Alfred Roy Carey, an aeronautical engineer of African American and Venezuelan ancestry. The marriage brought Patricia great happiness—it was a loving union—but it also brought her great pain; her family could not tolerate the marriage, and disowned Patricia. "I remember thinking, 'Where does this leave me?'" Mariah told *Smash Hits* magazine. "My parents went through a very hard time before I was born. It put a strain on their relationship."

Patricia and Alfred already had two children, a son named Morgan and a daughter named Allison, when Mariah was born on March 27, 1970. Her name came from a song: "They Call the Wind Mariah," from the musical *Paint Your Wagon*. Mariah would one day tell *People* magazine, "I think my mother chose the name Mariah because it would be a stage name." But the birth of their child couldn't save the marriage that was constantly being pulled apart by racial tensions. Patricia and Alfred divorced when Mariah was just three years old.

Mariah shared her mother's love of music, and from an early age, she used it to help her through the tough times. "I loved singing," she told *People* magazine. "I was singing since I was talking." After her parents divorced, she needed the comfort that music brought to her; her relationship with her father deteriorated quickly. "It's very difficult growing up in a divorced family," she told *People* magazine. "Everyone wishes they had a 'Brady Bunch' existence, but it wasn't reality for me."

Mariah shared more than a love of music with her

mother, she also shared her mother's talent. Patricia began to nurture that talent, giving her daughter singing lessons, training her to use and properly develop her voice. Patricia's friends from the New York City Opera would come to visit, and share their musical skills with Mariah as well. She would mimic the voices of performers she loved—everyone from jazz singer Billie Holiday to Stevie Wonder and Minnie Ripperton. At a young age, she also discovered Gospel music: she would accompany her paternal grandmother to her Baptist Church, where she soon learned the spirituals by heart.

But Mariah was still scarred by a feeling of "aloneness"—although she was happy about her singing abilities, and thrilled to be learning about music, and was still overwhelmed by a sense of not fitting in with the rest of the world. "I always felt different from everyone else in my neighborhood," she told *Ebony* magazine. "I was always so aware of my ethnicity—it was like, I had no place with anyone. My sister got the worst of it, because she had the darkest skin of all of us—kids would shout racial slurs at her, and she got beat up. It was tough." Mariah too suffered from the slurs and insults of her classmates. "When I was younger, I was an ugly duckling—I had really hairy eyebrows, that I didn't know you were supposed to pluck," she told *Ebony*. "Then I started doing stupid things to my hair—I used something on it that turned it orange. I was a mess. And I got teased all the time."

To escape from the tensions of every day life, Mariah sang and listened to the music she loved. She also began to experiment with poetry writing. And she spent a lot of time with her mother, who she always considered her best friend.

When she was a teen, Mariah and her mom moved to Long Island, New York. She attended Harborfields High, and adopted a "tough girl" attitude to overcome her insecurities. And although she never sang in school musicals or in the choir (choosing to keep her talents totally private), she blossomed in high school—she had lots of friends, and earned the nickname "Miss Mod." She shared her love of music with only one friend, Gavin Christopher, who she wrote songs with. When she was 16, her brother paid for her to make her own demo tape in a studio in Manhattan. At the studio, she met another friend named Ben Margulies, and the two began their own songwriting collaborations: Ben wrote the melodies, and Mariah composed the lyrics. When she graduated high school, she packed her bags and moved back to New York City, where she was determined to pursue her dreams of music stardom.

She immediately began to visit every record company in town, carrying the demo tape she had made with Ben.

She also worked a series of jobs to earn a living in the Big Apple: she was a waitress, a hatcheck girl and a hostess at a variety of New York City restaurants. She remembers it as a very frustrating time. "I would watch videos at home, and I'd be fuming," she told *Ebony*. "I'd think, why am I a waitress while these people are making videos?"

But it wasn't long before Mariah hung up her waitress uniform and got her first break—she was hired as a back-up singer for R&B performer Brenda K. Starr. "She helped me out a lot," Mariah told *People* magazine. "She would tell every one in the business, 'Here's my friend Mariah. She sings…she writes…'"

It was through Brenda, who had a record deal with Columbia Records, that Mariah met her mentor, the man who would eventually become her husband, Columbia Records' head Tommy Mottola. Brenda introduced Mariah and Tommy at a party, and there, Mariah slipped her demo tape into Tommy's hands. On his way home, he listened to the tape—and was blown away by Mariah's talent. He returned to the party to try and find her, but she'd already gone home. Through Brenda, he found Mariah, and when she called him, he told her, "I think we can make hit records." In December of 1988, she signed her record deal.

Mariah immediately began living in a whirlwind of activity. She traveled from New York to Los Angeles and back again, recording her debut album. She was not only singing, but she was writing songs with a variety of producers, who'd been hand picked by Tommy Mottola. She also continued to write with Ben, and their song, "Someday," was a favorite among everyone who worked on her debut album. The first single was chosen: it would be "Vision Of Love." "I was really thrilled with the way everything went on the first album," Mariah told *Smash Hits Magazine*. "It was just the way I'd hoped."

Once the album was completed, Mariah began the really hard work—doing publicity for the record and getting people to notice her. She was considered a "top priority" artist at Columbia Records, and she was soon appearing on TV talk shows and MTV. "Visions Of Love" hit #1 on the Billboard Hot 100 Chart, as did the album, titled simply, *Mariah Carey*.

With a hit album under her belt, Mariah was expected to tour—a notion that definitely did not please her. Since her high school days, Mariah had kept her love of music quiet, and had never gotten into performing in front of large crowds. "I'm not into performing," she told *The New York Times* magazine. "I have to make myself do it, because it comes with the territory." On August 5, 1990, she performed at the KMEL Summer Jam, which took place at the Shoreline Amphitheater in California—it was her first time singing in front of thousands of fans, and she did well, but it wasn't really something she was looking forward to doing again. Mariah was comfortable singing her heart out, but she would never feel completely at home on a stage.

At the 1990 Grammy Awards, Mariah's first album was showered with awards and accolades; she won Best New Artist and Best Pop Vocal Performance. But she didn't have long to savor her victories—Mariah was soon facing racial issues all over again. She was accused of being a "rip off," a white singer trying to "sound black." Mariah was shocked and upset about the attacks, which, considering her ancestry, hit her at a gut level. "I can't help the way I look, because it's me," she told *Ebony* magazine. "If people enjoy my music, then they shouldn't care what I am—it shouldn't be an issue. " For most fans, it certainly wasn't. Mariah's album remained on the Billboard charts, and her videos were constantly appearing on MTV.

The triumphs and the criticisms combined to invigorate Mariah, and she began to work on her second album almost immediately. Although most artists wait a minimum of two years between one record and the next, Mariah was ready get back into the studio. This time, Mariah teamed up with writer Walter Afanasieff, and again, found a writing partner that energized her. "I need someone really good to write with," Mariah told *Smash*

Hits magazine. "If I don't, I lose all my ideas." Most importantly, with this album, Mariah would be involved in every step of the recording process—writing, arranging, performing and producing. She was becoming a serious musical powerhouse.

The first single from her second album, "Emotions," (which would also be the album's title) was a huge hit, and so was the album. "It has a bit of an older-type vibe, a Motown feel," she told *New York* magazine. But the Motown feel obviously didn't make it with fans of Mariah's first album—*Emotions* didn't sell nearly as well as her debut album. But it fulfilled Mariah's expectations, and gave her the opportunity to show off her range: she sang songs that touched upon all her musical loves, from gospel to jazz. Another singer might have been worried about the sales figures for the second album, but Mariah wasn't—she was proud of what she'd accomplished. "I think it showed growth for me," she told *Smash Hits* magazine. "That was very important to me, to show the world what I could do."

She was also showing what she could do as a record producer in her own right, for other artists. She produced or co-produced six songs for vocalist Trey Lorenz, her former back-up singer, who became her protege. "I was so happy to help him, and I hope the music spoke for itself," she told *People* magazine. "It made me feel great to be able to help someone else make music."

Mariah had achieved professional greatness—her albums were huge hits, and she had hundreds of thousands of fans across the country. And in 1991, she also found personal happiness with her mentor and boss, Tommy Mottola. Since she'd signed to Columbia, there had been rumors of a romance between the head of the company and his musical find, but both had hotly denied them. Now it became clear that the two were indeed deeply in love. Although he was almost 20 years older than Mariah, Tommy was truly her Mr. Right. "We don't look at each other with a big age difference," she told *People* magazine. "We are just right for each other, and that is all that matters. That shines through all the differences, age and race. I think of him as a very special person, and everyone who knows us, knows we're right for each other."

On June 5, 1993, Mariah and Tommy made it official and got married. Mariah wore a Vera Wang wedding gown made of pale ivory silk, and a veil sprinkled with rhinestones. The couple honeymooned in Hawaii, then returned to New York refreshed and ready to begin working on another album.

That album was *Music Box*, and it would be Mariah's first new release in over a year (an EP, Mariah's *MTV Unplugged*, had been released the year before, and the single from it, "I'll Be There," was another huge hit single for her). The first single from the new album, "Dreamlover," soared to number one on the Billboard charts on September 4, 1993. It was Mariah's seventh number one single. The album also climbed to the number one position, and remained there for three weeks, slipped a bit, then returned to the top for another five weeks. The album was notable for it's dreamy, romantic ballads, natural enough for a young woman in love! "I sing from my heart, " Mariah told *People* magazine. "Whatever a song makes me feel at the time, I go into the studio and sing it the way I'm feeling it. Some people like it, some people don't—but that's the way I have to sing."

Mariah was well pleased with the album, but *Music Box* released a critical drubbing—music critics never seemed to appreciate Mariah's voice, and her efforts were often treated with a total lack of understanding and respect. *Time* magazine, for example, said of Mariah: "One gets the sense that Carey is squandering her chance at greatness." And her lyrics, the poetry that brought her so much pleasure, were often dismissed as trite, trivial and frivolous. But the negative voices of critics didn't stop fans from buying Mariah's albums in bulk.

Mariah was 23 years old when *Music Box* was released, and she was well aware that the album gave the world a glimmer of her artistic maturity. Now she was ready to show off her growth to the world; her first real tour was being planned, and Mariah was prepared to swallow her natural shyness, and to strut her stuff on stage. "I'm jittery, but I'm very excited about it," she told *Ebony* magazine. "I didn't start out performing in clubs, the way most people do. I feel like I'm being thrust out in front of millions of people. But I can do it." The tour was small—just five dates were scheduled. But it was a big enough of an event to send her legions of fans into a ticket-buying frenzy.

Again, she received critical backlash. CNN reported, "The reviews are in, and it's bad news for Mariah Carey." The criticism hurt, but Mariah used it to improve her show.

Mariah's concerts were filmed, and put together for an NBC-TV special which was aired during the 1993 Thanksgiving season. Thanks to the special, Mariah was introduced to more people than she could have imagined, and her high-energy show attracted even more fans.

In 1994, Mariah recorded a new version of the song "Endless Love" with Luther Vandross and, at the end of the year, she released a holiday album simply titled *Merry Christmas*. Mariah even wrote a few new Christmas tunes herself. "There was a priority for me to write some fun holiday songs," she told *CD Review*. "When you record a

Christmas record, it's important to mix traditional hymns with energetic, new songs."

Although Mariah seemed to be totally involved with work, she always took the time to express her concerns for others. In 1995, she got involved with The Fresh Air Fund, a charity that dedicates itself to sending underprivileged kids from New York City to summer camp in the country. In July of 1995, to honor her contributions and commitment to the organization, the fund renamed one of the camps Camp Mariah.

That year also brought new musical collaborations. Mariah worked with Puff Daddy on the song "Fantasy," and she was thrilled to have the opportunity to create music with him. "He's one of the best people out there," she told *Ebony* magazine. "He was my ultimate choice to work with." She also worked with the pop R&B group Boyz II Men on the single "One Sweet Day", a song that stayed at number one for and astonishing 16 weeks. Her next album, *Daydream*, was her greatest success yet—she even won over those critics, who this time around, sang her praises in a big way.

With such massive success, Mariah was suddenly in a position of great power in the music industry. She created her own record label called Crave, And she was determined that it would give new artists a chance to get their music heard. "I want to discover new talent that would otherwise end up nowhere," she told *Billboard* magazine. "I know exactly how it feels to have a tape and not to have anybody listening to it seriously. I had a lot of luck—a lot of upcoming talents have a hard time getting in touch with important people." Although Mariah had already been christened "The World's Best Selling Recording Artist," she was always looking to help newcomers to the music business.

In 1997, Mariah began taking acting lessons. She wanted to expand her horizons and was eager to enter the world of movies. She was also working on another album, and was deeply involved in the song writing process. But that year she also realized that she was not totally happy with her life, and it soon became clear that her marriage to Tommy was not working out. After four years, the couple split—although publicly, Mariah insisted it had ended in a friendly way. "I will always love Tommy, and he will always be a part of my family," she told *The New York Daily News*. "But right now, it's time for me to grow as an independent woman." The divorce would become final in 1998. Newspapers and magazines immediately began rumors of her supposed "romances," including a pairing between Mariah and New York Yankee shortstop Derek Jeter. But the truth was, Mariah was looking forward to finding herself.

Mariah took a major step with her new album,

Butterfly. The songs were more mature, self-assured and artistically more developed than any on her previous records. "My songs have never been this personal before," she told *Billboard* magazine. More importantly, she was taking care of her own career and making her own decisions, even regarding the skimpy, sexy outfits she chose to wear on stage. "I'm free and happy," she told *CD Review.* "The way I looked before, that wasn't me—that was a carefully devised picture. Now I sing what I want to sing and I look the way I feel."

In 1998, Mariah also released an album of her greatest hits, which included a new song, "When You Believe," a stunning ballad that appeared in the animated film *Prince Of Egypt.* It won an Oscar for best original song, and Mariah appeared on the Oscar telecast singing with the song's duet partner, Whitney Houston.

Mariah stepped into true diva-dom when she appeared on VH1's Divas Live, with fellow female powerhouse singers Shania Twain, Gloria Estafan and Aretha Franklin. Although many critics might use the word "diva" as a negative, describing a difficult, temperamental performer, Mariah showed the world what the word really meant—a strong, independent and truly talented woman, singing her heart out.

Mariah truly hit new peaks as an entertainer in 1999. She released *Rainbow*, an album that really broke a mighty record. The first single from that CD, "Heartbreaker," was Mariah's fourteenth number one single, a feat rivaled only by the Beatles (with 20 number ones) and Elvis Presley (with 18). She appeared in her first film, *The Bachelor*, with movie hunk Chris O'Donnell—she played one of Chris's ex-girlfriends, an opera diva. "It was just supposed to be a cameo role, but it got bigger," she told *Entertainment Weekly*. "It was a lot of fun." Mariah looks forward to continuing her movie career; two more films, *All That Glitters* and *Double-O-Soul* are in the works. She also revels in her musical accomplishments. She has sold more than 120 million albums worldwide, and has received bushels of awards, including World Music Awards, Billboard Awards, American Music Awards and her two beloved Grammys. And with the exception of her remake of the Jackson 5's "I'll Be There," every one of her number one singles was written by Mariah herself.

Mariah Carey is truly an artist who's destined to inspire millions of up-and-coming singers in the future. Her own future looks very bright indeed.

Bjork walks along the Great Wall of China during a day of sightseeing before a concert in February of 1996.

Bjork

AT FIVE FEET, zero inches tall, Iceland's own Bjork Gudmundsdottir is proof positive that the best things come in the smallest packages. For while her height in inches may be tiny, her talent is monumental.

Bjork was born on November 21, 1966, in the Icelandic capitol of Reykjavik. Her parents, Hilda and Gudmunder, divorced when she was only two years old, but the pair remained friendly and devoted to their daughter. Little Bjork often went to stay with her father and grandmother, Hallfridur, a former singer and artist—it was from her that Bjork first discovered her artistic soul. "She was a great woman," Bjork told *The Daily Telegraph*. "She gave me so many gifts."

But it wasn't her grandmother who first inspired Bjork to sing—that honor went to Julie Andrews, whose film, *The Sound Of Music*, was a blockbuster movie in Iceland when Bjork was born. By the time she was two, Bjork had learned all the English lyrics to the songs from the film—even though she couldn't speak a word of English. Her mother told *The Daily Telegraph*, "She repeated every word she heard. At family parties, she would spread her scarf on the floor and stand on it like a stage, to sing to us."

By the time she was six, Bjork was studying classical music on piano and flute, and at home, she was learning about the world of popular music. Her stepfather, Saevar, sang and played guitar for a group called Pops. Because of his experiences, he was quick to encourage Bjork, who was already showing signs of being a great performer. "I always knew who to go to if I wanted to hear a particular kind of music," Bjork told *Rolling Stone* magazine. "My stepfather, his sister and his two brothers were all musicians, and they were very carefree people."

Being carefree meant that Bjork was encouraged to use her imagination—and she had a wild one. She could entertain herself for hours, trying to teach her cats to fly. She would invent costumes using bed sheets. And she reveled in her family's "hippie" attitude; her stepfather's group played Jim Hendrix music, Eric Clapton music, and Bjork grew up heavily influenced by the music of the 60s, which celebrated individualism. "I've been called weird since I was four or five," she told *Rolling Stone*. "I made a decision then: I'd either live my life by what people thought of me, and to a set of rules I didn't really understand, or I could just do what I wanted."

By the age of 11, Bjork was a professional singer.

With her stepfather's help, she recorded a self-titled album in 1977. On it, Bjork sang a series of Icelandic folk songs and pop tunes like The Beatles' "Fool On The Hill"—but she also included a composition of her own, an instrumental number called "Johannes Kjaval," which was inspired by a famous Icelandic painter. Even at an early age, Bjork was highly self-critical, and she was especially hard on herself because she'd only penned one song. "It's wasn't my own work," Bjork reflected to *The Daily Telegraph*. "I wanted to be in control, to have it be all mine."

Although she was already a singer, Bjork continued living the life of an average schoolgirl. She was a cheerleader for her school's handball team, and she was an excellent student with an A average. In fact, she so excelled at math, that she thought long and hard about becoming an astronomer. But by the time she turned 13 she discovered punk and new wave music, and there was no turning back. She formed a number of bands, one called Exodus, another called Tappi Tikarrass and a third called Kuki. It was during her Tappi Tikarrass days that Bjork met and married musician Thor Eldon. Their son, Sindri, was born in 1986. (The couple divorced a few years later, but they remained very close; Thor was involved in the formation of Bjork's most successful band, The Sugarcubes).

With Kuki, Bjork recorded two albums before her 18th birthday. But the band broke up after three years. Bjork's only comment regarding the break-up was, "It was getting ridiculous." She never explained exactly what she meant by that, but the result was the end of Kuki and the beginning of The Sugarcubes. Bjork thought of The Sugarcubes as her weekend job—the band played light-hearted, fun, upbeat music at local clubs. But they caught the ear of the British music newspaper, *Melody Maker*, and suddenly, Bjork found herself enjoying her first taste of fame. Fans began trekking out to the clubs to hear her magnificent voice, and newspapers were interviewing her about her views on life, love and music. "It was like a holiday," she told *The Daily Telegraph*. "Free limos, free food, and you could bring all your friends. It was like a tremendous holiday." In 1988, The Sugarcubes released their debut album, *Life's Too Good.* Over the next four years, they would release three more albums. But in 1992, they split. Bjork blamed the break-up on financial difficulties.

With the end of The Sugarcubes, Bjork faced a major problem—she had no clue what to do next. She did know, however, that she wanted to sing and write songs. "I had all these songs floating in my head for years," she told *Rolling Stone*. "I knew I had to record them right at that moment, or I'd never do it." She traveled to England, and put all her energies into building a solo career.

It paid off. Her first solo album, entitled *Debut*, was a huge hit. It sold over two and a half million copies worldwide, and made Bjork a household name throughout Europe. Bjork had successfully mixed club and dance music—at the time one of her passions—with intense, deep and emotional lyrics. That mix turned into solid gold for the tiny, dark-haired singer with the soulful eyes and the big, big voice. Although Bjork had been a professional singer for years, she couldn't comprehend the whirlwind she'd created with her music. "I guess I was in the right place at the right time," she told *Smash Hits* magazine. "If I believed in astrology, I'd say that 1993 was probably destined to be good year for me."

It was typical Bjork understatement; in 1993, four of her singles became top 20 hits. Bjork face appeared on countless magazine covers throughout the world, and fans began to copy her hairstyles and her clothes. "I've been wearing these types of clothes since I was 14," she told *The Daily Telegraph*. "Suddenly someone decided they're in fashion!"

Bjork toured extensively in Europe, even though she wasn't completely comfortable on stage, in front of enormous audiences. "I would be a coward if I didn't do it," Bjork told *Smash Hits*. "I knew that performing live would be a difficult process for me." Bjork's naturally introspective, shy nature made it hard for her to sing in front of large crowds—she told *Smash Hits* that singing her intense songs before so many people sometimes felt like, "I was cutting out my heart."

Touring might have been unpleasant for Bjork, but writing songs and recording albums were not. She immediately began planning her second solo album. "Writing songs is a natural process for me," she told *Smash Hits* magazine. "If I don't write for a week, I go mad. It's like a deep need for me. I knew I had to make an album quickly."

Bjork's next album, *Post*, was a surprise to many of her fans. It was an exotic mix of jazz, techno-dance music, reggae, even big band sounds. The first single from the record, "Army Of Me," was included in the 1995 film *Tank Girl.*. Although many artists couldn't have pulled off the eclectic musical mix, Bjork made it work, and the album entered the British music charts at number two—it was kept out of the number one spot by Michael Jackson's *HIStory* album.

The video that was released from the Post album was "Its Oh So Quiet," which was directed by Spike Jonze—the off-the-wall artist who directed the 1999 film *Being John Malkovich*. The video became a monster hit—it featured Bjork dressed in a yellow sheet, dancing with Wizard Of Oz characters and animated fire hydrants.

The clip captured the imagination of fans and critics, and won a Music Week award. "When you blend my imagination with an imagination like Spike's there's no telling what's going to come out," Bjork told *Smash Hits* magazine.

The album was another monster success for Bjork, and once again the shy, almost elfin performer was back on concert stages all over the world—the schedule for her *Post* album tour was back-breaking. Clearly over-whelmed by the pressure, Bjork had to cancel four of her American tour dates due to nervous exhaustion. And she found it difficult to return to her beloved homeland of Iceland to rest—she was so well-known, she couldn't walk down a public street in her hometown without being chased by fans. Bjork turned to her family, including her mother and her son Sindri for support. "I'm not the most social person in the world," she told *Smash Hits* magazine. "Sometimes I think I could be perfectly happy staying at home with my family all the time."

In January of 1996, Bjork had recuperated from her nervous exhaustion and returned to touring in Britain, where she was treated like a musical goddess. Despite her personal dislike of performing live, she didn't disappoint her audience—her concerts were always showy, theatrical affairs, complete with intricate stage sets and other-worldly lighting. "I love magical realism on stage," Bjork told *The Daily Telegraph.* "I like to take the things that are surrounding us every day, and to make them magical—the sights and the sounds. When the audience reacts to my show, whether they cheer or boo and shout out insults, I feel I've accomplished something."

In February of 1996, Bjork experienced the backlash that often accompanies fame. She traveled to Hong Kong, where she was to be presented with a Brit Award for Best International Female Artist. She received it from Goldie, a DJ and performance artist from Europe, who she'd begun seeing romantically in 1995. Although she'd won the award before, and was accepting it from her boyfriend, she still flipped out over the enormous crowd that had come to celebrate the event with her. She cowered behind Goldie, too afraid to greet the audience face to face. She recovered her composure long enough to say a quick word of thanks, then she retreated behind Goldie once again.

Within the next few weeks, Bjork flew to Thailand for a performance. There was a media frenzy at the airport, and once again, Bjork seemed terrified by the crowds. To make matters even worse, Sindri was traveling with her, and Bjork, who was intensely protective of her son's privacy, was trying to shield him from the crowds and the bright, snapping flashbulbs of the cameras. When a British reporter greeted her by saying, "Welcome to

Bangkok," and seemed to move toward Sindri, Bjork flew into a rage, and the pair began a very public, and very physical, fight. The two were finally separated by airport security, but the damage had been done—Bjork's fight was the story on the evening news around the world.

The press and the critics, which had so far been firmly planted in Bjork's corner, now turned on her. *The Daily Telegraph* gleefully pointed out that one of Bjork's best known singles was a song called "Violently Happy," and wondered if the singer's image, that of a childlike, mischievous little girl, was really a cover-up for a violent, nasty temper.

And as if that wasn't enough, in September of 1996, an obsessive American fan committed suicide after sending a potentially deadly letter bomb to Bjork's home address. Bjork had no idea how to handle what was happening to her, and she withdrew from everyone and everything around her. Once again, the press criticized her, insisting that Bjork give a public statement about the tragedy—something she was not prepared to do.

The criticism was new to Bjork, and she was unprepared for it. Her record company, One Little Indian, released a statement to the press: "Bjork is just about to complete an extensive world tour, and is physically and mentally exhausted. She knows this does not excuse her behavior, but she hopes it explains why she acted so out of character." The singer herself remained in seclusion, although she did personally apologize to the reporter she'd exchanged blows with. She also told her fans, through various interviews, that she was having a hard time keeping her private life separate from her public persona. "The hullaballoo is not about you, but about the person you created," she told *Smash Hits* magazine. "When it comes to what I do—singing and writing and performing—it has so little to do with myself, and who I really am."

Despite all the hoopla, Bjork remained a bankable and much loved artist. Her song "Hyperballad" soared to number eight on the British charts, and the video, which featured two images of Bjork, one large and calm, the other tiny and overly-animated, became a fan favorite. But once again, the pressure of super-stardom seemed too great for the tiny singer, and she returned home to Iceland to spend time with her family. "All the craziness, it brought me back to the truth and made me real," Bjork told *Smash Hits* magazine. "I realized I had to cut the crap, and it settled me again. I had to get away from all the eyes watching me."

Ironically, her mother, Hildur, was also making records—her albums were intended for use when meditating, and featured the humming sounds of Icelandic singing bowls. Hildur welcomed her daughter home, but speculated about the toll fame was taking on Bjork. "There is a lot of stress involved, and Bjrok is the kind of person who needs to have her space and her family," Hildur told *The Daily Telegraph*. "She's not violent, like that scene at the airport—she's a gentle person. And while I'm proud of her success, it worries me that it's too much too soon."

In November of 1996, a group of artists put together an album called *Telegram*, which was a compilation of songs from the *Post* album. The artists on the album were an eclectic bunch, from the world's of techno-dance and hip-hop, and record confirmed that Bjork was having an incredible effect and influence on singers throughout the world. "I was touched to hear the album," Bjork told *The Daily Telegraph*. "I can't even put into words how it made me feel to hear it."

It seemed that Bjork had no real idea of how her inventive, mystical and totally unique sounds affected those around her. Although many critics considered her a "kooky chick," Bjork has always thought of herself as a song writer first, and she had a difficult time really understanding how her music has touched others. "I'm a singer," she told *Smash Hits* magazine. "It's sometimes hard for me to see how that can effect anything in the world. I'm very flattered that people are still into me after all this time, especially since I've never compromised and have been musically selfish to say the least. Even though I make music for myself, others seem to get something from it too. That's very gratifying."

Bjork remained in seclusion with her family throughout most of 1997, but as the year progressed she began to feel the need to record once again. She went back into the studio and began working on the songs for her third solo album, *Homogenic*. On June 6, 1997, she traveled to New York City for The Tibetan Freedom concert, where she previewed four of the songs from the new album. Then she returned to Iceland, once again regaining her strength from her homeland. "I went for a walk on my own, and I stayed on top of a mountain," she told *The Daily Telegraph*. "I saw the ice thawing, and I could hear the crackle of the ice. It was pitch black, the Northern Lights were swirling around, and I could see all the lights from all the towns of my childhood mirrored in the reflection of the clouds. It was really techno—it was truly inspiring. Iceland, my home, has always inspired me and my music."

Bjork traveled to El Madronal, in southern Spain, to record the rest of *Homogenic*. Unlike *Post* and *Debut*, this album would be totally self-produced—a first for Bjork, who had worked so well with others throughout the 20 years of her singing career. Bjork was able to totally give herself to her music, and to produce it without anyone else's input. Songs like, "All Neon Like," "Joga," "Hunter" and "Pluto" all explored Bjork's inner world and personal, while keeping true to her "really techno" sound. "The songs are about life and death and starting over again," she told *Smash Hits* magazine. "I'm writing completely different songs now, as compared to a few years ago. That character I was is definitely not me anymore."

In 1999, Bjork was once again exploring new worlds. She recorded a single called "Amphibian," which was included on the soundtrack of the film *Being John Malkovich*, directed by her old friend, Spike Jonze. And her contribution to the world of film was not limited to providing the background music—with her awesome sense of style, her unique look and her phenomenal talent, it was only a matter of time before Bjork would be approached to star in the film, and in 1999, she did. She made her acting debut in a movie called *Dancing in the Dark*, which co-stars international film legend Catherine Deneauve, and will make its first appearance at the Cannes Film Festival in the year 2000. The soundtrack to the film includes several new Bjork songs. The movie is a musical, set in the 1940s, and to prepare for it, Bjork had to take dancing lessons. But Bjork didn't enjoy the process of film making, and told The Daily Telegraph she won't be switching careers anytime soon. "I hated acting.

I actually felt like I was cheating on music."

Bjork always returns to her music—and she does it in a positively 90s way: she's a total computer head, and she does most of her song writing on her computer. "I'm obsessed with my laptop!" she told The *Daily Telegraph*. "I think one should allow electronics to be absolutely electronic, and proud of it. Technology and music should never have to be separate."

In 1999, Bjork also explored her political side when she joined a protest over a power plant that was scheduled to be opened in Iceland. Bjork was clear about her stands on the environment, and is a deeply committed member of the group Friends of the Environment. "To sacrifice nature for modern technology is an obsolete concept," she told The *Iceland Daily News*. "Iceland's environment is one of the things that makes it so unique throughout the world, and it must never be damaged or destroyed." To show her commitment to her environmental beliefs, Bjork and the Icelandic band GusGus wrote a song called "It Is Not Up To You"—the proceeds of the single's sales will be used to create an economic development fund of Iceland's rural areas.

Although Bjork is thoroughly committed to her political principles, she is first and foremost a singer. On New Year's Eve, 1999, Bjork performed at a concert in Iceland to celebrate the coming millennium. She is preparing another world tour for 2000, and planning to release another album in 2001. "I receive letters from fans, asking when I will be releasing new songs," she told *The Iceland Daily News*. "It always surprises me, how much people like my music, and how much they look forward to it. Sometimes, I feel the pressure of fame, and I think I can't do it anymore. But I always do—that need to write songs, that need to sing them, comes over me, and I can't say no."

Bjork is planning to release music from her new album over the Internet—an idea she finds exciting. "I think it's excellent," she told her audience during a recent Internet chat on IRC. "It's a simple and natural elationship between the listener and the person who makes the songs."

All in all, Bjork remains an artist who is true to her music. "As I get older, I find it is more important to make my songs reflect what goes on inside my head," she said during her IRC chat with fans. "My music is simply my relationship with myself. I never looked at it as a career—music is my emotional survival. It keeps me from going insane."

Index